I0697051

I Governor of Minnesota

An Ideography – from **EPIC** to **DO GET USE**

Bob "Again" Carney Jr.

Copyright © 2022 Bob "Again" Carney Jr.

All rights reserved.

ISBN: N/A
ISBN-13: 9798431470721
Library of Congress Control Number: N/A

DEDICATION

To my Parents

CONTENT

I Governor of Minnesota

INTRODUCTION

IMPORTANT: This book was written before Russia invaded Ukraine. I'm rolling out another book specifically addressing that situation – this book's back cover has a **Post-Trump Pledge** featured in that book. This book is likely to be revised multiple times based on the rapidly developing situation in Ukraine.

This book is foundational for my 2022 campaign for Governor of Minnesota (but also for an "interim" campaign for Congress, more on that -- and possibly future campaigns.) The campaign is framed as a kind of remake of an earlier, then-famous (but now forgotten) and surprisingly successful campaign: Upton Sinclair's 1934 run for Governor of California.

Mr. Sinclair and I have one similarity – we are both writers. His output was prodigious by the time he ran for Governor of California. Mine – not so much (but I'm catching up!) However, as a writer, and a Republican, I have in Minnesota something similar to Mr. Sinclair's writing in this respect: over a little more than a decade the

Star Tribune has published around 25 or 30 of my commentary articles on their Op-Ed page. As a result, I have become well-known, and arguably somewhat famous, to the entire Minnesota political establishment, who, by and large, are all my readers. For this reason, I do have an unusual but established political base. Simply by filing for a state primary I start with about 10,000 or 15,000 highly educated and informed voters inclined to support me.

Chapter one digs into Mr. Sinclair's 1934 campaign. At that time, constructing the infrastructure needed for a statewide political campaign was very challenging. Today, by contrast, we have the incredible speed and reach of e-mail, the internet, youtube.com, social media generally, and the unusual structure and economics of today's self-publishing opportunities. This META-mess make it theoretically possible for a campaign to "go viral" in ways that simply were not possible in 1934. I'm hanging my hopes for accomplishing something remarkable on the simple fact that today's technology is (potentially) so much more empowering, and fast-acting, than what Mr. Sinclair had to work with.

Of course, the current "rap sheet" on "us" – on the whole "USA" – is that we're also incredibly divided… maybe hopelessly divided. Without flat-out denying reality, I'm committed to challenging this assumption also. More specifically, I think there is potential for many dialogues, including a Republican-Socialist dialogue – something this book is heavily weighted towards promoting. My hunch is that a lot of people are looking for a way out of today's division. My plan is to offer a way out – starting with this book.

Briefly, I am both a long-time Republican, but also a charter member of the "Never Trump" camp. In a Star Tribune commentary shortly after the 2016 Republican Convention I advocated for a kind of Electoral College rebellion, designed to offer alternatives to the proposed "Trump-or-Clinton" deal. From that time forward, I've been convinced that Trump is manifestly unfit and unqualified to President. In 2017 I published <u>Break Glass Impeach Trump</u> – laying out a "new" Constitutional theory and showing both why and how I thought he could be impeached. New is in quotes, because this is a theory I've been working on since self-publishing my first book on it in 2000 – in fact the last three chapters of my 2017 book are taken from that earlier, 2000 book. I'll be rolling out another impeachment book shortly – addressing both the context of the January 6th 2021 <u>insurrection</u> (that word is *not* in quotes… it's underlined!) and advancing several new Constitutional approaches to both impeachment generally, and Trump in particular.

Republicans simply must face up to the Trump disaster. He is an insurrectionist who must not be allowed to appear on a Federal ballot again.

The recent Russian invasion of Ukraine has brought this issue to a boil. We are seeing the consequences of having a dangerous authoritarian in control of a large country with nuclear weapons. This is sobering a lot of people up. And let's remember – there is strong if not overwhelming evidence that the 2016 U.S. Presidential election was stolen… not by Trump, *but by Putin and Russia.* We have got to face up to this. I am personally committed to doing everything I can to ensure that Trump is never on federal election ballot again. He must be stopped.

Shortly before I wrote this introduction, a personal tragedy struck: First District Minnesota Congressman Jim Hagedorn died of cancer – he had been battling it since shortly after his 2018 election to Congress. My sympathy goes out to his wife, Jennifer Carnahan, and the Hagedorn family.

However, politics does not stop. There will be a special election for the Minnesota First District Congressional seat. Although I'm not a resident of the district, residency is not required. I have filed for the Republican primary for that seat. My only issue will be advancing my specific ideas to deal with former President Trump --   more specifically, how to ensure he cannot appear on the ballot in 2024. The First District primary is May 24th, 2022. If elected, I would serve from the August special election – to be held on the same day as the Minnesota primary election for Governor (yes, I know it seems weird but you can run in both elections on the same day) – until the next Congress takes office in early January 2023.

What this really amounts to is that I'm kind of applying for the position of a long-term substitute Congressman – someone to "cover the class" until the next election. On the one hand, Trump is such a pressing issue that a Republican who *can* and *will* deal with this issue is sorely needed. But on the other hand, I think in the long term the First District deserves to be represented by someone who is from the First District, and has roots in the First District… not someone who is merely "legally qualified" to run, as I am. So… even if I'm elected, I do not plan to seek a full term – instead, I would simply run in both the August primary for Governor *and* the special election for the Congressional seat. I'm now working on a short book dedicated specifically to the issues regarding Trump that I'll be raising in the Congressional campaign.

Is the medium the message? Kinda

"The medium is the message" is one of Marshall McLuhan's many famous phrases ("Global Village" is another). Although the field of media studies had existed for decades, in the "popular mind" McLuhan rose to a de facto position as its "guru-founder" simply because his writing and ideas about it became so widely popularized. Before McLuhan came along few people knew much about media studies… many had never heard of it.

McLuhan is not a topic in this book beyond this introduction (he's mentioned only briefly) – but we should consider that the level of division in America today should be directly associated with a long-term shift in the forms and character of different *kinds* of media that dominate the political arena. The most obvious long-term change is from print-based newspapers, magazines and books to high-emotional-impact forms – from newsreels and radio to TV and internet-based forms.

A big part of my effort is to encourage a shift away from short-form, passion-saturated "image based" media to long-form, dispassionate "text based" media. Of course the book is the prime example of the latter. I think that when reading, we humans tend to think more clearly and with more nuance.

It's that simple. We need not go into McLuhan in any detail – the essential point has been made.

This also ties in with what I'm presenting as my official campaign slogan:

Turn Off – (formerly "Turn On")

Tune Out – (formerly "Tune In")

Drop In – (formerly "Drop Out")

This will jog the memories of many older folks, who will realize it is a "triple negative" of the slogan promoted by Dr. Timothy Leary – introduced to us with a William F. Buckley quote at the end of Chapter 11 as the self-described "Pope" of a new religion premised on claims of possible "spiritual benefits" from using psychedelic drugs – LSD in particular.

Upton Sinclair's EPIC agenda vs my agenda: DO GET USE (chapters 3-6)

End **P**overty **I**n **C**alifornia – **EPIC** – was the centerpiece of Upton Sinclair's 1934 campaign for Governor. This is covered in Chapter 1 – Chapter 2 presents the idea that something similar can happen in Minnesota. Regarding Sinclair's 1934 **EPIC** campaign permit me to just make a bare bones point: This was the height of the Depression; California was hard hit, like the rest of the country. Sinclair's main idea was simply to put people to work in factories and on farms – producing things they could both use and sell. It was sensible and popular as a basic concept.

My campaign has a similar acronym approach, but with three acronym words – **DO GET USE** -- not just one. This "triple acronym" is also presented in detail -- in Chapters 3 through 6 (Chapters 4-6 are each about one word; **DO**, **GET** and **USE** respectively.)

The essence of **DO GET USE** is based first on the idea that a lot of progress has been made since the Great Depression. America does now have an economic safety net that was lacking back then. But I think we should emphasize a basic idea that seems being lost sight of amidst "basic income" chatter. It still makes sense to first expect people to **DO** something – typically this means work, but with needed exceptions for those who can't work. In return for work, people **GET** something – typically income… but I'm willing to consider other options. Finally, people **USE** what they **GET** – they provide for themselves and their families. I think this **DO GET USE** idea should remain the foundation for our economy.

But I also understand that everyone, Republicans included, must also seek new and better ways both to provide for "the public benefit" and to safeguard and improve our environment. That's addressed in **Chapters 4 through 6** – which lay out plans for doing this. A lot of this is based on the opportunity to use technology in new and better ways. As just one example, **Chapter 6** introduces one of my inventions – a global thermostat that I foresee as being used to literally set the temperature of planet Earth while also generating enough solar electricity to pay for itself. How's that for audacious? Please note: this is ultimately something subject to scientific verification. My challenge to everyone is: show me where I'm wrong in my facts and reasoning.

Chapter 5 (out of order) introduces more radically innovative thinking about how we can develop an infrastructure using both Electric Vehicles and vehicles powered by hydrogen gas using Internal Combustion Engine technology. This can also be zero emission – we can capture and recycle Carbon Dioxide produced by vehicles burning fossil fuel, and we can recycle that Carbon Dioxide into synthetic liquid fuels that can also power existing ICE vehicles. How's that for some innovative thinking? I have a book length version of this plan (review copies are in production) that I'll be rolling out… sometime.

Chapters 7 through 10 are focused on what I would do as Governor – but more generally on how I would approach the opportunity to lead Minnesota, (and the USA, and the world) in some new and badly needed directions. By now this should be clear: I'm a "big picture guy." But something else should also probably be clear to a lot of open-minded and practical people: I'm probably also incompetent.

Let me start by just flat-out conceding this point – but permit me to also point out that unlike many other incompetent people, at least I *know* I'm incompetent. This is serious – I read an article once (long ago, can't find it) claiming that most incompetent people *don't know* they're incompetent. Self-knowledge is a first and necessary step. BTW, if you can find that article on the internet (I think it's late 1990s or early 2000s) please let me know.

A serious point is being made here, and a serious issue is being addressed. In our system of government, we have both a Governor and a Lt. Governor. We have legal provisions that under certain circumstances the Governor can turn over the day-to-day operation to the Lt. Governor. Quite simply, my plan is to find a running mate who *is* clearly competent to be Governor and turn the operation over to them. This will leave me in full control of the "bully pulpit" – but more time to advance all of my great ideas. And here's the crucial point: I won't be bungling and screwing up the day-to-day operation. That's my plan.

Chapter 11 – the "Big Enchilada" – The other chapters are from "snack size" to "full meal size." This one is the "Big Enchilada" – about a fourth of the book. Here's a bare nub description of my effort: to trace a theme of intentional social and behavior control forward from Upton Sinclair to the present. My own perception is that as human beings we have all become so totally dominated by institutional social control that this dominance itself must be surfaced as the single most important reality we need to confront. I see this as across-the-board. People may "align" with some preferred paradigm of dominance – but we don't seem able to escape some sort of dominance – even if it's partially or almost totally a matter of choice or personal preference. To get beyond our society's hyper-divisiveness I think we all need to confront this reality.

Chapters 12-14 and the Afterwards – These address some needed topics, but except for Chapter 13 can be left aside for now. Chapter 13 is a promise: "I will work to

keep Trump off any future Federal election ballot."
Because I have filed for the Minnesota 1ˢᵗ Congressional
District special election Republican primary, at this point
I'll just ask you to keep an eye out for a short book I'm
working to crank out on this ASAP.

I hope you enjoy this book and find it useful. I'll be
making it available as a free e-book on Kindle about every
month. I'm also planning to produce a shorter version
that will be free during the campaign. If you have
questions or any reaction, please don't hesitate to contact
me.

Bob "Again" Carney Jr.,

Minneapolis, March 21, 2022

1 -- "THE CAMPAIGN OF THE (LAST) CENTURY" -- UPTON SINCLAIR'S 1934 RUN FOR GOV OF CALIFORNIA

The 1934 campaign for Governor of California of up-to-then Socialist Upton Beall Sinclair Jr. is a perfect case study for two big themes of my own 2022 **DO GET USE** campaign for Governor of Minnesota. That's why I've chosen to model this book, and the campaign, around that earlier campaign.

Two of my goals are to begin a Republican-Socialist dialogue, and to consider how during periods of great stress, major American political parties can respond by being dramatically re-shaped and re-formed.

By the way, launching into this, the second longest chapter… we should get something out of the way. Many people confuse Upton Sinclair with Sinclair Lewis, a Minnesota writer (born Harry Sinclair Lewis in Sauk Center) and the first American to win the Nobel Prize for Literature ("NPL") – in 1930… right at the start of the

Great Depression. Are we coming full circle?... the most recent NPL winner, Bob Dylan, is also from Minnesota. I'm not sure what to make of the fact that he cancelled his own first name but we do know this: when Mr. Lewis, Harry Sinclair started out, Mr. Upton Sinclair was widely known… and as we know all publicity is good publicity. Could it have been the publisher's idea to drop "Harry" and go with "Sinclair?" We also know this: Mr. Lewis, Harry Sinclair wrote the phenomenally successful <u>Main Street</u> (set in Gopher Prairie, modeled on Sauk Center MN.) More to the point for us today he also wrote <u>It Can't Happen Here</u>, a 1935 expository novel about the rise to power of an "American Hitler" (sound familiar?...) But trying to avoid snark and inside jokes when you read it is like trying to daintily eat a chocolate-filled eclair. <u>It Can't Happen Here</u> was an obvious fictionalized warning about Louisiana Governor and then Senator Huey Long, seen by many to be a potential populist challenger to FDR, and someone who really *might* have successfully challenged FDR and really *could* have been an American version of Hitler or Mussolini. Huey Long was killed -- apparently by a ricochet shot fired by his own bodyguard -- during an attack in September 1935, shortly before <u>It Can't Happen Here</u> was published. Had he not died, that book could have become a far more pointed and important warning about what *can* happen here in America.

The parallels between our two Sinclairs (and our two "American Hitlers") are many, interesting, and also serious

– but again, this book is centered on Upton Sinclair, who also wrote many novels. <u>The Jungle</u> (a 1906 novel) is Upton Sinclair's best known book -- but his prolific writing featured many books that are best categorized as factual expositions and journalism.

Until his 1934 run for Governor of California at age 54 Upton Sinclair had been an active and prominent Socialist for decades, and a candidate for public office multiple times. However, following his own account, he faced constant difficulties and obstacles while attempting to communicate his ideas. One of his best known non-fiction works is <u>The Brass Check</u> (1919)… rooted in his own experiences and chronicling how Sinclair saw the media of his day -- newspapers and magazines, but also book publishing. The book's title is derived from the phrase "Brass Check" – which denoted a token purchased at a brothel. Sinclair saw journalists of his day as prostitutes, working for business organizations whose dependence on paid advertising dictated what they could write and publish. Sinclair's relationship with the *New York Times* is superficially similar to President Trump's ongoing symbiotic dust-ups. More generally, Sinclair might have kicked himself had he discovered the availability of the term "fake news." We'll come back to consider some surprising and striking similarities when comparing Sinclair's critique of the entire "American Establishment" to how today's Trumpers might view it.

But while the establishment reactions reported on by Sinclair and the still-in-power establishment's reaction to the Trump Legions are in many ways strikingly similar, the issues Sinclair raised with the establishment of his time are vastly and thoroughly better analyzed and thought through.

Here's a relevant excerpt from Wikipedia's The Profits of Religion article, describing the series that includes The Brass Check: "The book [The Profits of Religion] is the first of the 'Dead Hand' series: six books Sinclair wrote on American institutions. The series also includes The Brass Check (journalism), The Goose-step (higher education), The Goslings (elementary and high school education), Mammonart (art) and Money Writes! (literature). The term 'Dead Hand' ironically refers to Adam Smith's concept that allowing an 'invisible hand' of individual self-interest to shape economic relations provides the best result for society as a whole."

The "Dead Hand" series is an extradentary, across-the-board indictment of major America institutions at that time, including an exposition of interlocking networks of relationships among American elites that controlled them. Another part of my reading has been an on-line PhD Thesis critiquing Sinclair's writing. On the one hand I'm impressed with the breadth and thoroughness of Sinclair's writing, but it also appears that there is still no comprehensive critique of it – either an attempt to audit it factually, or an attempt to systematically present a comprehensive critique. This looks to be a great project for future historians. In Chapter 11, I offer up a critique of events from Sinclair's own career forward, including his one-man charge against the fortified reality of the American establishment of his time. For now, let's just leave it this: anyone who does what he did should expect to make a lot of enemies, should expect entire institutional establishments to try to ignore and suppress him, and should understand that he has published a mountain of ammunition that will be used against him if he does something as crazy as run for Governor of California. But to this must be added: through it all, and in the years that followed up to 1934, Sinclair maintained cordial personal relations with establishment figures throughout America, of all political persuasions, including President Theodore Roosevelt, who returned his phone calls to the White House, and had him over for dinner while in office (it has been reported that Roosevelt privately viewed Sinclair with contempt.)

This brings us to the main topic of this chapter – Sinclair's one-man full-frontal-tilt assault against all the windmills in the World… well… in California anyway. As we'll see, he came surprisingly close to succeeding, and his influence on the future of American politics was unquestionably lasting.

Sinclair's EPIC campaign (<u>E</u>nd <u>P</u>overty <u>I</u>n <u>C</u>alifornia)

As the 1934 election was coming into view, Sinclair was approached by many who encouraged to run for Governor -- but as a Democrat, not a Socialist. American politics was in turmoil. Socialists had been closely linked to attempts at socialism in the Soviet Union, which in turn were criticized. Two devastating famines, resulting in millions of deaths in 1921 and 1933 were certainly affected by drastic change going on in the Soviet Union – some argue the later famine was genocide. Could that history have been an influence on Sinclair in switching to the Democrat – as a means of disassociating himself from accumulating Socialist baggage? The 1933 famine was not widely publicized, but it is certainly possible Sinclair might have learned much about it through his own extensive network of sources – including information that was not being publicized through established media channels. The Democratic Party, led by President Franklin Roosevelt was open to considering new ideas of all shapes and sizes. We've already seen Roosevelt was also facing an emerging populist threat from Louisiana's Huey Long with his "Every Man a King" theme.

To jump ahead a little: after he had won the California Democratic primary, Sinclair took a continental train ride to a September 5th two hour meeting at President Roosevelt's Hyde Park New York home. He described that meeting to the press: "A few crumbs I was able to give them – harmless things such as what the President had said about 'The Jungle' – how his mother had insisted on reading it to him at the breakfast table – and naturally it had spoiled his appetite." (p 87 of the "how I got licked" book.)

Now to rewind our story; Sinclair agreed to run, and (naturally!) launched his campaign with a book laying out his plan for **EPIC** – End Poverty In California. To briefly summarize (and necessarily to say some obvious things) Sinclair saw the major problem in California as massive unemployment; as a solution he proposed what he called "production for use." His basic idea was that if unemployed people could be provided the means – farm land and factories to grow food and produce basic products – then they could both eat, and have enough to provide themselves with the basic needs of living. In this way, they would not be poor, and would not be unproductively unemployed. Since factory production and farming were significantly depressed, both land and manufacturing capacity were available. Without getting into detail, Sinclair laid out a financing scheme by which the State could obtain the use of needed land and manufacturing capacity, and could then put unemployed people to work. This, in very summary form, is the guts of Sinclair's **EPIC** plan as laid out in his book.

His personal campaign activity consisted of many public meetings and radio appearances. Of course, his book was also widely distributed. Many **EPIC** chapters were formed all around the State, to explain to people the basics of the plan.

One experience Sinclair recounts is a kind of general raising of awareness. It seems throughout California, everyone thought that everyone else was doing ok. As he started to ask people at public meetings "how are you doing" – and asked for a show of hands – many people who had felt isolated began to realize that a lot of people were in the same boat with them.

Continuing to skip almost all detail, the **EPIC** movement grew and spread quickly. A weekly newspaper reached a circulation of over a million. Unionism and the New Deal were important to the campaign – the 1934 West Coast Longshoreman's Strike led to unionization all West Coast ports. The 1934 Longshoreman's strike triggered many others around the country, including the Minneapolis general strike of 1934. These strikes shaped the Roosevelt Administration's position that there was a vital difference between specific strikes involving labor-management economic disputes, and general strikes with a larger political agenda. FDR's administration supported the former but condemned the use of the general strike as a tactic.

The August 28th Democratic primary result was a decisive victory – here are the results reported by Sinclair's post-campaign book: "Sinclair, 436,000, Creel, 288,000, Wardell , 48,000, Milton K. Young, 41,000; and a few thousand for each of the others."

This caused universal panic among the entire California (and national) establishment. Quoting Sinclair, "A former Socialist had captured the Democratic nomination by the biggest vote ever polled in a California primary" and would be on the November general election ballot. He had met with President Roosevelt for two hours – the President (we learned later) had read Sinclair's book presenting the **EPIC** plan and was keenly interested. Below is a post-primary cartoon from Sinclair's post-election I, Candidate for Governor: And How I Got Licked book (p 75, following his account of the meeting with Roosevelt.)

In that post-election book Sinclair recounts what in his view was an unprecedented, vicious and lavishly funded smear campaign launched by the entire panicked establishment. The book has a number of cartoons (this book's cover is a modified version of one) that ran in California newspapers – whose response to Sinclair was certainly "payback" for The Brass Check. Sinclair recounts: "At my conference with President Roosevelt at Hyde Park on September 5, he had volunteered the statement that it was his intention, on or about the 25th of October, to come out "in favor of production for use"; and I had remarked that if he did that, it would elect me."

(p 200.) While he recounts eagerly awaiting the "Fireside Chat" the President did deliver about that time, and his disappointment when Roosevelt didn't come through. Sinclair wrote: "Of course I was dished. No use to say a word more; the newspapers had me in their jaws, and would shake me as a terrier shakes a rat… The 'New Republic' wrote editorially that nothing Roosevelt had done as President reflected less credit upon him than his treatment of Upton Sinclair. I find that most of our **EPIC** people feel such bitterness; but I argue that this is not justified. In the first place, the President had made no promise to me; he had made a simple declaration of intention, and he had a right to change his mind. I had done nothing for him; and he had an election to win, and power to hold. I was an unknown quantity, and how could I tell what he might spring next?… but assuredly his mother had never read The Profits of Religion to him; and if somebody brought him one of those leaflets from California, full of garbled quotations, might he not reasonably decide that I was a dangerous partner on the political trapeze-ring?" In short, Sinclair understood the difficult position his campaign had put Roosevelt in, with the New Deal a precarious and still-being-thought-up emerging reality.

The November general election result was an impressive achievement for such a radical undertaking, but one that came up short. Sinclair reported (p 223, parties and percentages inserted in brackets): "To finish the story of the election and its results: the official figures show that Merriam [Republican] received 1,138,000, [48.9%] I [Sinclair, Democrat] received 879,000, [37.8%] and Haight [Progressive] 302,000 [13.0%.] It thus appears that Merriam is a minority Governor by a small margin."

But life goes on… and so did Sinclair's "How I Got Licked" book (p 224): "The victory of Merriam was not a victory for reaction. One of our achievements during the campaign was that we forced the old gentleman completely out of his lifelong position. Before he fight was over he had announced himself as 'heartily in accord with President Roosevelt's policies.' He proved it in a genuine and touching way – by dumping onto Roosevelt's shoulders all the gravest of his problems – old age pensions, unemployment insurance, relief for the destitute, and the thirty-hour week. [¶] This sudden conversion of a Republican of the school of Mark Hanna to the most alarming of brain-trust ideas suggests a curious problem… The Governor-elect waited only two or three days after the election before taking over the **EPIC** Plan. He announced in a speech that the unemployed must have work, and that, much opposed as he was to the idea of letting them produce for barter, he would adopt it as a matter of temporary necessity. He reiterated his promise for a thirty-hour week, and incredible as it may seem, he broached a State income tax."

So… a happy ending: Sinclair and all his dangerous ideas were soundly defeated!?

Well… no. And that's the point. Ideas have ways of getting bound up, modified and marching on.

There's a lesson for me and my fellow Republicans here – the Democrats (Socialists) have lots of good ideas – all we have to do is steal them and genetically modify them a little. Let's go for it!

This is partly – but *only* partly -- tongue-in-cheek.   As an illustrative point: counter-culture guru Abbie Hoffman wrote <u>Steal This Book</u> – which ironically became a best-seller (assuming that shipments to bookstores less returns were all bought.) As a Republican, I don't want people to get into bad habits by stealing books… or anything (Hoffman was clearly a troubled person.) Of course, the book you're reading – <u>I, Governor of Minnesota</u> -- is periodically being made legally available for free during the campaign -- but you can also make a campaign contribution by buying it.

Rather than attempting some kind of an audit as to how exactly Sinclair's **EPIC** plan played out, let's just return to one of the two themes made at the beginning, then make a point, and finally wrap up. Here's the theme: "…during periods of great stress, major American political parties (there have been only two since the Civil War, all attempted upstarts have been extinguished) can respond by being dramatically re-shaped and re-formed." At the time of the New Deal a lot of that was going on with both parties. We are in another national crisis today -- so this process is of course going on today… as best it can. We need to study and shape how our major parties change.

On to the final and serious point we must consider: When we start thinking and talking of stealing ideas, we get into some pretty serious difficulties pretty fast. Many have noted a significant and seemingly hard-to-explain overlap: people who supported both Bernie Sanders and Donald Trump. This is too easily blown off as just a reflection of similarities in personality and style – bombastic and pugilistic. But there are also significant overlaps of ideas, values, and a generally wary posture towards institutions. These overlaps should be explored as another way to account for this phenomenon. This is also why a Republican-Socialist dialogue is important.

To wrap up: although I'm convinced that he was, and would be again, constitutionally dangerous as President, Donald Trump (who stole the slogan "Make America Great Again" from President Reagan) has prompted a lot of shaking-up and rethinking (some but not all of it good!) in both parties. Here's the bottom line: "trafficking in ideas" is really less like stealing and more like panning for gold. As with California gold diggers, our task is to find the nuggets and throw out the rest – but in a far more environmentally friendly way than the original '49ers.

----

*Footnote for Chapter 1.

Here's what Upton Sinclair wrote about Mr. Lewis, Harry Sinclair, in Money Writes: "Twenty years ago I had what the New York newspapers were pleased to call a 'Socialist colony'; and one day there turned up at this place a run-away student from Yale University. Harry Sinclair Lewis was his name, and we called him 'Hal'; he was tall and lanky, red-headed and talkative, merry, and as we learned later, observant. He applied for the job of tending our furnace without knowing anything about it; and as none of us knew any more than he, we let him. He sat round our four-sided fireplace in the evenings and got a complete education in every aspect of the radical movement, which was far more useful to him than anything he could have got at Yale."

"Now he is the most famous of American novelists, and I shine in his reflected glory. About fifty per cent of the strangers I meet tell me how much they enjoyed 'Main Street'; or else they frown, and I know they are blaming me for 'Elmer Gantry.' Even newspapers do it; the editor of a religious paper has just damned me for having challenged God in a Kansas City church. I am getting uneasy for fear the recording angel may have got it wrong in his records, and what will I do if I wake up in hell?" [ed: Upton Sinclair continues to dish on… er… tries to correct and reform?... Mr. Lewis, Harry Sinclair… viewing him as marginally useful to the cause -- and in correspondence holding him to account for filtering out Socialist themes and ideas in his writing. Everyone's a critic… even writers! Shocking… zzzzzzzzz. For his part, Mr. Lewis, Harry Sinclair fires back in ways too numerous to list in It Can't Happen Here… two must suffice here: Upton Sinclair is presented as a supporter of the "American Hitler" president, and is then appointed by him Ambassador to England. It's hard to pinpoint where and how exactly It Can't Happen Here ceases to be one giant inside joke.]

To bring Sinclair's critique more into focus, a few pages later, he critiques Eugene O'Neill, America's second NPL winner; here's the start: "If you think that my understanding of proletarian art is Socialist lectures disguised as novels and soap-box orations preached from a stage, then let me hasten to say that these early plays of O'Neill are part of what I want and have got. Here is a man who writes about the sea, from the point of view of the wage-slaves of the sea, with full knowledge, insight, and pity; yet, so far as I can recall, there is not one word of direct propaganda, hardly even of indirect. Let a man show capitalism as it really is in any smallest corner – as O'Neill has done in 'Bound East for Cardiff' – and the message of revolt rings from every sentence."

Regarding the idea that all publicity is good publicity Sinclair demonstrates his awareness of this on p. 214 of Money Talks: "… the well-established principle that every knock is a boost." [p 214] in the world. We know this for sure: it has the highest tuition.

2 -- A 21ˢᵀ CENTURY REPUBLICAN "SINCLAIR II" IN MN? – IT **CAN** HAPPEN HERE

Of course, the "It can happen here" part of this chapter's title derives from Mr. Lewis, Harry Sinclair's <u>It Can't Happen Here</u>. But any further similarity ends at the outer boundary of possibility – as you'll see, one of my main purposes is to end any possibility that ex-President Trump could be restored to power in 2024.

My hope is that the plans and ideas I'm advancing will bear fruit in a version of what Upton Sinclair accomplished in California in 1934. But before getting to those plans and ideas, this chapter is a brief nuts-and-bolts survey of why our internet environment and Zoom, when combined with Minnesota's culture, political heritage, and election laws present a uniquely favorable set of circumstances. Here's the brief, bullet point survey:

- **Internet / Zoom / social media** – nothing complicated here… Upton Sinclair's campaign required a mammoth effort in constructing a physical campaign infrastructure – meetings, a weekly publication, organized chapters. Today, while possible and offering great potential, all of that is <u>simply unnecessary</u>. If this goes viral, it will be through an existing infrastructure for distributing ideas that is fundamentally unlike the one that so strongly resisted Upton Sinclair's efforts… over decades… to distribute his own ideas.

- **The Minnesota Republican Party** – this is also virtually unique among state parties. It's tempting to get bogged down about this; but vitally necessary *not* to get bogged down. There will be more on this – a lot more— as my campaign continues. For now, let me just offer this very blunt assessment: **First**: while the media's emphasis has been on how elected Republicans are forced to bow and scrape to Trump, few people are aware on a nuts-and-bolts, inside-politics basis, of how complete Trump's takeover of the party's machinery has been all across America. This will be elaborated on in Chapter 13. **Second**: it is a huge mistake to think Trump's base can ever move beyond Trump as the result of an incessant attack mounted against *both* them *and* Trump. The best approach is to sincerely welcome Trump's supporters to the Republican party -- as I do -- and, to the greatest extent possibly, ignore Trump, focusing on issues instead. **Third**: if this process of moving beyond Trump can't happen in Minnesota, it probably can't happen anywhere else in the country. Things have to start somewhere.

- **The Minnesota Political Contribution Refund** – This is unique to Minnesota. People can contribute $50 to a State campaign or a State party… couples can contribute $100… and they will receive a dollar-for-dollar refund from the State. **Note:** This is viewed by me and many others as *fundamentally different* from public campaign financing. No person can live in Minnesota for a year without paying $50 in taxes, one way or another, directly or indirectly. Recognizing that reality, $50 of what was collected from you, or on your behalf, is simply being returned to you. This unique program makes it possible to finance grass roots campaigns. Over the years it has been highly successful as an alternative to big money in politics. I don't think I can raise much campaign money, nor do I *need to* for an effective campaign. But our unique PCR program will help greatly. This should be implemented nationwide, at both the Federal and State level.

• **Minnesota has an open primary** – Voters do not register by political party in Minnesota. Anyone can vote in any party's primary; the only restriction is that you cannot "mix and match" – voting for one party's candidate for one office, and another party's candidate for a different office. Let me be both blunt and candid. One of the purposes of this open system is to enable political parties to respond to the changing thinking and beliefs of voters. As noted at the start of Chapter 1: "during periods of great stress, major American political parties can respond by being dramatically re-shaped and re-formed." Open primaries are part of Minnesota's overall approach to ensuring this response is possible, and stays possible.

This nuts and bolts, inside-politics is important for you to know. "A 21st Century Republican 'Sinclair II' in MN?" It *can* happen here. In Minnesota. More to the point – it might not be possible anywhere else.

But should it happen?

The rest of this book is my pitch to you – explaining why I think it should happen, and asking you to help make it happen.

3 – THE CAMPAIGN OF <u>THIS</u> CENTURY – **DO GET USE**

As we've seen, Upton Sinclair's campaign was framed around **EPIC** – End Poverty In California. **EPIC**, in turn, was founded on the idea of production for use. The idea was that if people had the means of production -- land and factories – they would produce much of what they needed, and could buy the rest by selling the useful things they produced. In Sinclair's view this wasn't happening because people didn't *want* to work – or were unwilling to work – but because they lacked access to two of the three vital "factors of production" in the jargon of classical economics – Land and Capital (factories.) They themselves were the third factor of production: Labor.

The general idea that people should be able to work resonates with both Democrats and Republicans. From FDR's New Deal forward, our whole political system has been responding to the problem Sinclair focused on in his **EPIC** campaign. We continue to have recessions. But we have developed a "safety net" to provide for people during those recessions. We've also developed an entire "welfare state" – in recent years totaling close to $1 Trillion a year at the federal level alone – when you add up the cost of a long list o programs, with sometimes bewildering requirements, including both incentives and disincentives to work. It's not a perfect system by any stretch of the imagination. But it does represent a response that has developed over what is approaching the one century marker since Sinclair's **EPIC** campaign.

DO GET USE sums up what I see as both the widely accepted alternative before the Great Depression, and the still-preferred default situation since them – especially among Republicans.

The idea is simple:

First, you **DO** something – typically this means you work. But as suggested above, for some people in various circumstances, working may not be involved. Instead there may be many different kinds of **DO**… generally establishing that some eligibility condition(s) have been met. However the **DO** step is carried out, we then go to the next step.

Second, you GET something in return – typically wages or a salary. But as people become independent in various ways and to various degrees, the **GET** part can take many forms.

Third, you **USE** what you got. This typically means you buy things with your wages or salary.

Other approaches have been and are being proposed. Notably, in the most recent Presidential Campaign, then-Democrat Andrew Yang pitched his Universal Basic Income ("UBI") plan – offering an alternative to the **DO** part of my plan. Under Yang's plan, people would receive $1,000 a month as a basic income. Everyone could still work – although that fact didn't attract as much attention.

The point of my **DO GET USE** plan is two-fold. **First,** it builds on the existing system America has had since the founding – a system that Republicans universally still support today. Let's keep in mind that even during the Great Depression, when unemployment went above 20% -- the basic pre-Depression **DO GET USE** system was still working for over three fourths of the country.

Second, as we'll see in the next three chapters, each of the three elements branches out to a plan to deal with future challenges we face (both America and the World.) Here's a brief introduction to each of these.

DO -- Demand Organizing

Our starting point here is supply and demand – the two most important curves (but also sometimes lines or squiggles) in all of economics. A third assumption is key:

perfect competition. This means that for basic commodity goods – agricultural crops are the perfect example – there are so many suppliers (individual farmers) that no one producer can influence the price that the market sets. That price is the point where the supply curve and the demand curve meet.

This is a great in theory – but reality is far more complicated. Gigantic oligopoly or monopoly suppliers is only one of the most obvious problems – our standard attempts to control this with anti-trust law are failing and floundering. But I think something else is at work, and I haven't heard it discussed explicitly. This is an information-and-resources imbalance between supply and demand – which affects both what is produced… and maybe this is more important: what *isn't* produced. I've developed a theory of **Demand Organizing** that I think offers great potential to address this imbalance. And here's a final key point that's typically especially important for Republicans: this **Demand Organizing** can be carried out *without* relying on government to *do* anything. Rather, the key is to ensure that Government cannot *prevent* this **Demand Organizing** process from happening. With **Demand Organizing**, I think our enduring and dominant **DO GET USE** system can be made to work much better. This is the subject of the next chapter. Now, on to the **GET** part of the plan.

GET -- Green Energy Technology

Both **GET** and **USE** look to the future, and to our need to address environmental and climate change challenges. Absent my alternative approach there is much to be examined and questioned about the Democratic/Socialist Green New Deal approach. I am challenging this head-on. But as you'll see, by offering a constructive alternative approach – and one that can in fact be both economically profitable and hyper-synergistic – the need to refute the Green New Deal plan vanishes. Instead, I claim the burden of proof shifts – others should try to show either why my approach won't work… or why their far more intrusive and expensive approach is better. I'm concentrating on elaborating on my approach and the advantages it offers.

The general idea behind **GET – Green Energy Technology** – is that there are technological solutions to our environmental and climate change challenges that do not require us to stop using carbon-based fossil fuels. Hold on all you woke liberals… hold on… I know that sentence is like having a Doctor hit your knee with a sledgehammer. I'm providing one major example, coming up at chapter length, but also available in book form. It's called **JIT Energy**. JIT is short for Just In Time – it's built around the idea of delivering small doses of energy – as either a battery charge or as burnable hydrogen gas – to vehicles *while* they are moving. One big feature of this plan involves the ability to capture Carbon Dioxide emitted from Internal Conmbustion Engine ("ICE") vehicles, and then use solar energy (both heat and electricity) to recycle the CO2 into liquid fuels that can be poured right back into your gas tank. By building and using the **JIT Energy** system, we can *continue* to use both fossil fuels and ICE engines – which… it turns out… have many advantages, including the fact that their main output, heat energy, can be put to all kinds of uses if we're only determined to be practical about doing it. So… that's the blurb-length pitch… elaborated in Chapter 5, and also at book length.

USE -- Utility Solar Energy

This is a planet-sized idea that, I submit, emerges from careful consideration as a fundamentally better basic alternative to the so-called Green New Deal. It is based on a provisional patent I filed in 2018, which is currently being examined by the United States Patent and Trademark Office ("USPTO".) The patent is for… (I doubt you're ready for this but please bear with me) a *Global Thermostat* that can within a small but sufficient range literally set the temperature of planet Earth. This system can also pay for itself by generating incredible quantities of electricity using existing (and new – more are coming) solar panel farms. Because this system can set the temperature of planet Earth – either up or down -- it can handle both Global Warming, and any possible new Ice Age. Rather than elaborate here I can only say: read

Chapter 6. Here, I'll just add one more outlandish claim, and then explain the "Utility" part. The further outlandish claim is that my system can be used to generate electricity from solar panel farms at night.

If you're concerned that I'm just plain nuts, please skip ahead to Chapter 6. Otherwise, patience! – it's coming up soon enough. For now let me just add two points: First, my claims about the *Global Thermostat* invention are fundamentally a scientific ones – they can be proven and/or disproven at any level of detail. Second, the rest of what I'm proposing in **DO GET USE** *can* all be carried out (but with less impact and at greater cost) with or without the *Global Thermostat* element. You can simply discount the idea of a *Global Thermostat* entirely... as two fanciful, or too... whatever... skip Chapter 6, and read the rest. While the *Global Thermostat* element is severable from the rest of the plan – the Utility element of Solar Energy, and thus the whole **USE** element – is integral to the plan. I can only add that my USPTO examiner are talking and corresponding. We'll see what happens on that front.

Now for the "Utility" part. We've already noted that our childishly simple Supply/Demand economic model has some major problems and flaws. During the last century however, some major economic progress has been made in the area of utility regulation. The basic problem is that left to itself, a monopoly business finds ways to extract profit that no individual producer can match when there is perfect competition. However, there are sometimes significant economic advantages in having monopolies. Distributing things like water, electricity, and natural gas, are classic examples. It simply doesn't make economic sense to have $N = 6$ different companies… each with their own network of pipes or wires. Municipal and other government-owned utilities are one way to attack this problem… but establishing regulated utilities is another way. The idea behind a regulated utility is to regulate the rates that can be charged to customers; based on an economic analysis of each business. The economic analysis determines what it costs to run the business, and then adds in a "normal" profit – not allowing the "monopoly profit" that an unregulated monopoly would figure out how to get.

My Solar Energy *Global Thermostat* plan assumes there will be a start-up phase which will of necessity involve tapping into capital markets to fund development and early, low-volume production in some capitalist countries. However, each country is free to contract independently – meaning that Socialist or quasi-Socialist countries can finance start-ups in ways of their own choosing. However, once scale is reached, the assumption (again depending on the country) is either continued financing involving the Government, or on a utility basis. Relying on this mix of economic bases means that in the United States Solar Energy from the *Earth Thermostat* plan can be on a "cost-plus" basis – allowing for the cost of producing it, plus a "normal" profit. The idea is to produce an abundance of solar generated electricity. **Note:** in all countries this can be provided to consumers on a sliding scale – everyone can receive what amounts to an energy version of Andrew Yang's Universal Basic Income idea. We could call it something like a Universal Energy Income. Whatever… naming and branding are details down the line.

Again, this is all in Chapter 6.

To wrap up: **DO GET USE** is founded on our enduring and current system – most Republicans will probably view this as something between a continuation and a restoration. But as **Demand Organizing, Green Energy Technology**, and **Utility Solar Energy** unfold, the plan will also address structural flaws with a system based on what are frankly childish assumptions about the real-world interaction of supply and demand. This intelligent and market-disciplined approach to green and solar energy will also prove to be a better one than the current Green New Deal mentality.

That's the pitch. The next three chapters will equip you to form at least a preliminary opinion.

4 – **DO** = DEMAND ORGANIZING

We tacitly assume a kind of equality of Supply and Demand in a competitive free market economy. I think this is a mistake. Suppliers, often individually, but almost always as industries, have some overwhelming advantages in controlling both what individual products, and what "systems of products," are offered to consumers.

Here's the distinction: One individual, particular car is a product. By contrast, our entire transportation network, including roads, railroads, vehicles of all kinds, gas stations and convenience stores, and more… is a "system of products." Here's the main claim: As a group, Suppliers are organized. They control what consumers can buy, and they appear to be heading more and more to de facto control – an entire economy of oligopoly Suppliers. This can explain why our stock market has done so well since COVID – midsized and small competitors lack the resources to roll with change the way giant organizations have. The market can "see" what this is leading to in terms of an economy dominated by profit-sucking oligopolies.

When it comes to specifying and designing what products will be available, with what features and at what prices, "Demanders" and "Suppliers" are definitely not "created equal." We the Consumers -- "Demanders" – often think dreamy, vague, brief thoughts about "what do I want?" Then we might turn on the TV… browse some device… vote for Bernie… join the Yang Gang… pop a tall cool one… go to a Trump rally… whatever! Meanwhile, "Suppliers" are far more disciplined and serious: they have engaged entire private armies of mercenaries to study… plan… plot… and conspire against *We the People*!

Adam Smith, <u>The Wealth of Nations</u> author (or "the Dead Hand guy" as Upton Sinclair might say,) offered up this famous quote in his 1776 book (yup, it came out the same year as the Declaration of Independence, emphasis added): "People of the same trade seldom meet together, even for merriment and diversion, but the conversation ends in a conspiracy against the public, or in some contrivance to raise prices."

Tens of millions of Americans are engaged daily -- as commute2zoom mercenaries -- in a vast "Supplier-wing Conspiracy."

Collectively "Suppliers" have an enormous investment to protect. Some pesky MBA with good marketing instincts could result in the extinction of giant companies, or even entire industries. It happens. Economist Joseph Schumpeter called this process "Creative Destruction." In America alone for-profit corporations really do employ armies of people – probably tens of millions – who work full time studying all the pieces of all the "Demand Puzzles" and all the different ways these pieces – including millions of pieces that hardly any "Demander" even knows about -- might be put together and… this is crucial: how potentially threatening products can be *prevented* from ever being put together.

A supplier oligopoly has extensive control over its entire relevant "systems of products." As one example, an industrial sector like "Transportation" is in a very powerful position to influence – we'll… let's get real… to control and dictate: how our network of roads is built and maintained, and what kinds of vehicles are allowed on them. By the way, vehicles are often subsidized… as an example: for city busses the Federal government typically pays 80% of the capital cost paid by state and local entities. Of course the zoning for commercial properties that abut and surround roads and highways is also controlled. The list of puzzle pieces goes on.

A big part of this Supplier Dominance is that, as a group, consumers… let's call us "Demanders" – simply don't know about possible new products, or "systems of products" – that we probably *would* demand if only we knew we could. However, if we as consumers… "Demanders" – become knowledgeable and organized, we can, as groups, obtain control of needed Intellectual Property, productive resources -- and this is crucial -- Government authority, to both produce and permit new products and systems of products that can promote the General Welfare – to hearken back to our Constitution's language.

By-the-way again, in his time Upton Sinclair documented this whole process of control with massive, overwhelmingly convincing detail. We're in agreement as to this reality – however, in my view the group of "controllers" has changed – this is detailed in Chapter 13.

A Primer on Public Benefit Corporations

Public Benefit Corporations are a new kind of legal entity – a kind of hybrid between a for-profit corporation and a non-profit corporation. Non-profits are often called "organizations" -- they typically have the internet suffix .org instead of the for-profit suffix .com. This obscures the fact that "non-profit" and "for-profit" are both forms of corporate organization.

The main difference from the pre-Public Benefit Corporation era is that for-profit corporations were (and still are) widely if not universally understood to be formed with the primary (many still think exclusive) intent to make money for their owners – either one person or a group of shareholders. This was the fundamental difference with the non-profit corporation form, which in theory exists solely to provide various kinds of public service and social benefits.

You can contribute after-tax money to any for-profit corporation. Send Apple a check for $100 and feel good about yourself! But of course almost no one does this. However, while your sent-from-love check to Apple is not tax deductible, your contribution to a non-profit corporation *is* tax-deductible. This difference in taxation reflects the traditionally different purposes of the two corporate forms. For-profits exist to earn money for shareholders (a private purpose) – Non-profits exists to provide a public service or social benefit (a public purpose.) Many people believe non-profit corporations can in some ways provide public services and social benefits either more efficiently or effectively than government can, or in unique ways that governments cannot do.

Two other critical differences follow from the explicit public-service or social-benefit purpose of Public Benefit Corporations as compared with traditional for-profit corporations. First, in purposefully fulfilling a Public Benefit duty, directors and officers of a Public Benefit Corporation are legally immune from legal threats and lawsuits they might face from shareholders of a traditional for-profit corporation. Second, and this follows from the first point, Public Benefit Corporations can be structured in a way that can make them more or less immune from the threat of a hostile takeover, launched by a giant predatory for-profit corporation. Such takeover threats can succeed against a traditional for-profit corporation if a predator makes what is literally an "offer you can't refuse." A minority of shareholders of a traditional for-profit takeover target *can* legally demand that such offers be accepted – backed up with the credible threat of a lawsuit. But because a Public Benefit Corporation has a public purpose, directors and management can simply say: "Thanks, but no thanks – that rail car load of gold you want to send us would defeat the purpose of our company's existence."

This new Public Benefit corporate form has the potential to be a powerful way to carry out Demand Organizing. The next chapter will give one more detailed illustration of this – but there are many more major possibilities out there.

Demand Organizing freedom vs government coercion

Here's what I see as the heart of our dilemma. **First:** we want to preserve the idea of people free to act effectively in a voluntary way, trying to extensively and successfully resist the kind of vast, Supplier Organizing Structural Conspiracy that Adam Smith warned us about. But **Second**: our attempts to do this by using the powers of government – both criminal and anti-trust law, but also the whole regulatory Administrative State spawned from the New Deal -- just haven't worked very well.

I see **DO… Demand Organizing…** as a better option. Here's the key point and the key difference: unlike the "please-Government… save-us-from-ourselves!" approach, **Demand Organizing** can be best accomplished by working carefully, prudently and judiciously to get government *out of the way* – to make sure that government cannot and does not *prevent* us from providing real and massive social benefits.

This approach is not anti-government – rather, it is essentially anti-authoritarian.

To see this, let's briefly consider the Green New Deal ("GND") approach, and the Build Back Better ("BBB") approach from my admittedly wary and biased Republican point of view.

The essence GND/BBB is founded on the idea that national politics is a giant battle over control of the machinery of government. If the "woke Left" gains all the levers, they can fund giant government programs, with intermediary job security and sinecures for millions of Progressive Authoritarian bureaucrats to carry out their plans, which they confidently believe go beyond vague, full-of-hugs-and-bugs, untested ideas. The Trumpers are also seeking to gain control of all the levers… but they have a fallback position: controlling only some of the levers is enough to thoroughly gum up everything the "woke Left" is trying to do. This is my best attempt… my best pitch… at trying to sum up what I see going on today. It's my story and I'm sticking to it.

We'll revisit this idea of **Demand Organizing** after providing some more context – an example of a plan for **Green Energy Technology** – the "**GET**" part of **DO GET USE** – in the next chapter.

To wrap up, let me reemphasize what I see as the "**DO**" advantage: **Demand Organizing** can put Supply and Demand on a far more level playing field, *without* using the coercive powers of government to *make* people do *anything.* In short – it offers the prospect of de-escalating the battle over controlling the levers of power.

5 – **GET** = GREEN ENERGY TECHNOLOGY

There are many possible kinds of **GET -- Green Energy Technology.** They can be simple and small-scale, but they can also be systems involving entire industrial sectors. The example we'll consider in this chapter goes big – I call it **JIT Energy.**

JIT is biz talk for **Just-In-Time** – an idea originally applied to manufacturing. The theory is that business can be more efficient, and prices can be lower, when we try to get away from having large inventories. Instead, we produce everything on a Just-In-Time basis. Entire supply chains can be coordinated so that everything arrives in bite-sized quantities.

Of course, recently America's supply chains have been getting yanked big time. But this isn't a new problem. I remember when I was in Biz school – and drove with my Dad to Texas and back over Winter break (AKA Christmas.) On the way back, a big ice storm came through – but we decided to push on home instead of staying in our motel in Iowa for one more day. Between mid-Iowa and the Twin Cities I must have seen ten or twenty eighteen wheelers in the ditch – they had all slid off the way-too-slick freeway. I thought they all must be under pressure to get their loads delivered Just-In-Time to wherever those loads were intended to go. Lesson remembered: things can and do go wrong – not All The Time – but frequently enough. We must always be mindful of problems and pitfalls.

Still, there is a lot of merit to the Just-In-Time idea – enough so that it is still being widely applied. In my upcoming book-length plan, I apply it to the entire Transportation sector. Here's the background, the basic idea, and the many incredible merits it offers.

Electric Vehicles (EVs) are the big buzz today – but they were a big buzz back in the early 1900s too. One of the reasons they lost out to Internal Combustion Engine ("ICE") vehicles was the sheer bulk and weight of batteries. Today, Tesla's EV batteries are about 1,100 pounds, they're the heaviest and most expensive component.

It's also possible to run ICE vehicles using hydrogen gas as fuel. Hydrogen is incredibly explosive, and the byproduct is H2O – better known as water! If we can successfully use hydrogen gas to power ICE vehicles there is tremendous potential to reduce pollution. However there are also delivery and storage problems with hydrogen gas. Everyone remembers the horrific photo of the Hindenburg Blimp disaster.

Still… let's optimistically push on – to see what possibilities there might be.

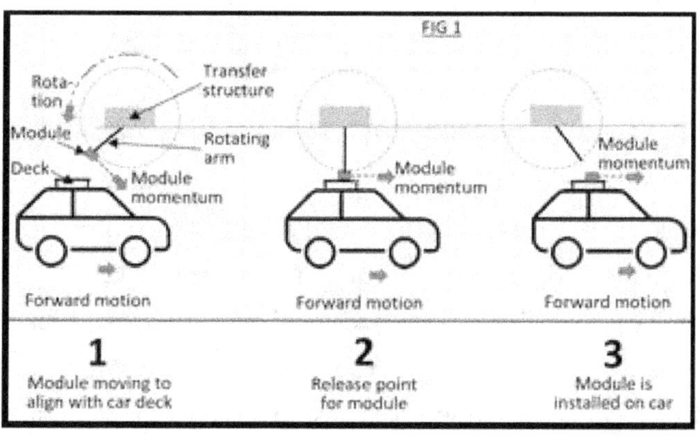

FIG 1 (above) illustrates the basic idea behind **JIT Energy.** We can deliver and retrieve modules of energy, and of captured Carbon Dioxide and hot liquid, to and from the tops of vehicles while they are moving. These modules are exchanged between vehicles and transfer structures, which are mounted above a road right-of-way. Let's skip the details, only noting that at the point of exchange the momentum of the vehicle and the module are identical – they have the same direction and the same speed – this enables a smooth and safe transfer.

The **JIT Energy** plan supports two types of delivered energy – either small supplies of electric charge (in a battery) or a small quantity of hydrogen gas – both are sufficient only for a few miles of travel. But with frequent exchange stations, we only *need* a small quantity of energy to power vehicles. Again, we're skipping details that are covered in the book-length version of this.

Another key feature of the **JIT Energy** plan is to remove potential energy from vehicles on a Just-In-Time basis. This is in two forms. **First,** we can capture and remove the exhaust from an ICE vehicle running on fossil fuel. The first advantage of this is that it doesn't go into the atmosphere – so the system solves our pollution problem. But there is another and equally incredible advantage to doing this. Burning hadrochemical liquid fuel (AKA gas and diesel) is a *reversible* chemical process. This means we can recycle the Carbon Dioxide exhaust that we capture, processing it into various optional forms of liquid hydrocarbon fuel – which can be pumped right back in to the gas tank of a conventional ICE vehicle. In effect, we can "unburn" the fuel, and then "reburn" it – and this cycle can be repeated.

Of course, there's a catch – you need heat and electricity to "unburn" the fuel – to recycle it into liquid fuel that can be reused. But both heat and solar electricity can be and are supplied from the Sun. We simply need to develop an infrastructure that ultimately powers ICE vehicles with solar energy – using what amounts to endlessly recyclable fossil fuel.

Of course (again) the rap-sheet indictment of ICE technology features this fact: compared to EVs, ICE vehicles are incredibly inefficient. Because all ICE technology works by converting heat energy to mechanical energy, it is limited by the Carnot cycle – a physics-based analysis demonstrating the upper limit of mechanical energy that can be obtained from any heat-to-mechanical-energy process. As a practical matter: we are all driving boilers. Our boilers produce *some* mechanical energy – typically 20% or 30% -- that's why we buy them and use them. But we literally throw away most of the energy an ICE engine produces. As air moves through the radiator, it dissipates the heat energy. This is *how* we throw it away.

While the Carnot cycle is an entirely real, science-based limit, our conventional way of looking at this situation is deeply flawed in two ways. **First**, we ignore the fact that so much of our electricity – you know… the stuff that goes in EV batteries – is also produced by heat engines. Big power plants are more efficient that vehicles – but between the inherent inefficiency of the heat-to-electricity process and the infrastructure needed to deliver electricity – we aren't much better off.   And by the way, all nuclear power plants are also essentially heat engines.

We're also ignoring a second crucial fact. We have all kinds of uses for heat energy. While winter is our most obvious example, heat energy can be used to catalyze the process of recycling our recaptured Carbon Dioxide into liquid fuel we can put right back in gas tanks. Finally, ICE vehicles can be viewed as a general-purpose means for exchanging various forms of energy. We can use them while they're sitting to produce electrical power – potentially reducing or even almost eliminating the need for electrical grids. We can heat homes and buildings with the heat energy they inevitably produce. All of this is accounted for in my **JIT Energy** system. We can exchange modules containing heat energy that ICE vehicles (mobile boilers) have (inevitably) produced while they were moving. Instead of using a radiator to throw it away, ICE technology can be designed to use basic principles of heat exchange to capture the energy, and transfer it from the vehicle the same way we transfer the captured Carbon Dioxide the vehicle is emitting.

Let's conclude with this final point: Today -- *right now* -- we have an entire worldwide infrastructure to produce and service ICE technology. The current Green New Deal plan declares this is all obsolete and we need to get rid of it. My **JIT Energy** plan declares: "*No* – ICE technology is *great* – we just need to redesign the whole system to make better use of the heat energy it produces, and to leverage the fact that it can perform multiple changes of energy states that are largely location-independent."

So… that's the intro-level introduction of **JIT Energy** – but permit me re-emphasize, this is presented in considerably more detail in my book on the subject.

Now, back to…

A *Demand Organizing* perspective on *JIT Energy*

Do we need government to convert our world-wide transportation sector to my proposed **JIT Energy** approach?

No… we don't.

This can be done entirely on a for-profit basis, relying on the free consent of people who want to make it happen. While many Democrats will find such a prospect appealing, I think an even larger percentage of current Republicans, and people who are more and more open to becoming Republicans will like this.

Our current system of capital markets, combined with our communications technology and the Public Benefit Corporation is fully sufficient to do this. Beyond that, it can probably accomplish this transition more quickly and efficiently – with far less total "political heat" required – than could be done by using government to try to ram it through.

My plan for using the Public Benefit corporate form to carry out this plan is presented in my book on the topic – along with a significant elaboration of **Demand Organizing**.

That's a wrap for this chapter.

6 -- **USE** = UTILITY SOLAR ENERGY

Chapter Preface

Similar to **GET -- Green Energy Technology** there are multiple options and variations for **USE -- Utility Solar Energy**. However, in this chapter I'm going to focus on one basic technical model and one basic political-economic-financial model, which I believe is directly applicable for America, but is also generally appropriate for all mixed-capitalist western-style democracies.

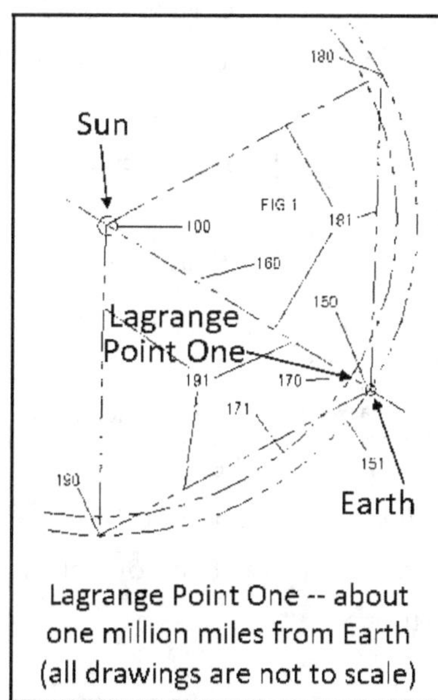

Lagrange Point One -- about one million miles from Earth (all drawings are not to scale)

The basic technical model is my currently patent pending "Earth Thermostat."

What is Lagrange Point One?

This is simplified – many details are ignored. Here we go. The two illustrations for this chapter are from one of my patent applications. The first illustration (previous page) highlights the Sun, along with the Earth and

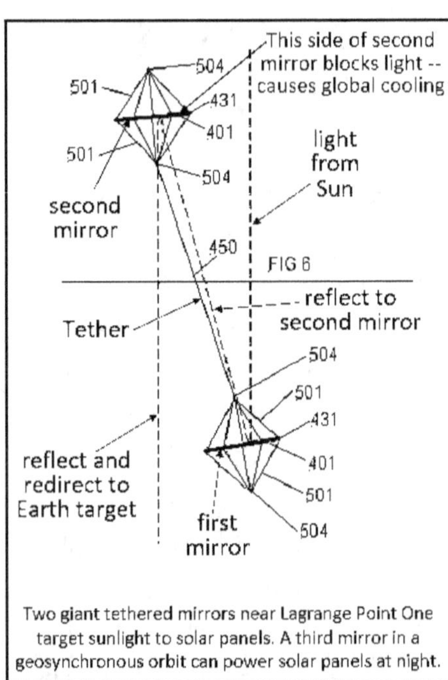

Two giant tethered mirrors near Lagrange Point One target sunlight to solar panels. A third mirror in a geosynchronous orbit can power solar panels at night.

Lagrange Point One – we'll start calling it LP1 now -- which both orbit the Sun. As it orbits the Sun, LP1 remains about one million miles from the Earth, and about ninety-two million miles from the Sun. LP1 also remains on what we'll call an "Earth-Sun axial line." One point on the axial line is at the Sun's center of gravity, while a second point orbits with the Earth's center of gravity – like the hand of a clock that you might see on a courthouse.

This brings us to the special property that makes us interested in LP1. At LP1, the Sun's gravity, the Earth's gravity, and the orbital centripetal force all balance, and cancel. The result is that anything we put at LP1 will tend to stay there – orbiting the Sun and always remaining at the same distance from the Earth and the same distance from the Sun.

If we want to put anything easily and sustainably between the Earth and the Sun, LP1 is the only place we can put it. But LP1 is really more of a circular area on a plane that is perpendicular to the Earth-Sun axial line. For our practical purposes, this circular plane version of LP1 is centered on the axial line, we'll use a radius of very roughly 8,000 miles. At all points on this circular surface an object won't be pulled towards either the Sun or the Earth, but both gravitational fields will have a slight force pulling it towards the center of the circle. The point is this: LP1 circle has a huge area (comparing with terrestrial objects) – over 200 million square miles.

Climate Change is a huge challenge. The older term for it -- Global Warming -- is still applicable and useful for us. The biggest problem with CO2 (Carbon Dioxide) and other greenhouse gases is that they cause Global Warming. The most discussed solution to greenhouse gases has been to both prevent adding more to the atmosphere, and to remove greenhouse gases that are already there. This could reduce and eventually eliminate Global Warming.

But other approaches are possible. One is to increase the Earth's albedo – a measure of how much incoming sunlight is reflected by the Earth's surface. Painting surfaces white, or adding a shiny surface, increases albedo. When more sunlight is reflected back into space this makes the Earth cooler.

Another and more direct approach is to put objects at or near LP1 that will manage the total sunlight reaching the Earth. There are two basic approaches. **First**, we can simply reduce the total sunlight reaching the Earth. **Second**, we can use pairs of giant mirrors to redirect and target the sunlight that reaches the Earth.

We have proof of concept for the first approach from Dr. Roger Angel, an Astronomy professor at the University of Arizona and a MacArthur "genius grant" winner. Dr. Angel published a paper in 2006, proposing putting a cloud of very light refractive disks in the 8,000-mile-radius LP1 circle, covering about 1.8% of the area through which sunlight passes on its way to Earth. The trillions of Dr. Angel's one-meter-wide disks would cause sunlight to miss the Earth, reducing Global Warming. In 2006 he was talking about a cost of a few trillion dollars, or less than half a percent of World Gross Domestic Product -- and a time frame of less than 25 years.

The U.S. patent I've applied for is based on a different approach, but one still rooted in managing the total energy reaching the Earth from the Sun. The next illustration is also from my patent, showing how a system of two tethered mirrors in the LP1 circle can be used to redirect sunlight to an Earth target – or another mirror orbiting the Earth.

As shown in the second illustration (back a few pages,) two giant mirrors are tethered together – each is surrounded by a framework (501). Small ion engines can be placed at both ends (504) at the top and bottom, to maintain tension in the tether and to manage the position of the entire structure. Sunlight is reflected from the first mirror to a second mirror, which redirects it to a target on Earth or orbiting the Earth (a third mirror.) Targets can include solar panel farms. The intent is to be able to produce enough solar electricity from these giant structures to pay for the whole system – all managed by a for-profit Public Benefit Corporation.

With giant mirrors orbiting Earth we also have another amazing opportunity – we can generate electricity from solar panels at night. Yup – they can run 24/7. And because light is directional, no one will see the sunlight being directed to the solar panel farms. Of course the ability to run solar panel farms 24/7, with increased intensity directed to them at all times, will greatly improve the productive efficiency of the solar panels.

Support for this system can include people who don't think Global Warming is real, but who are willing to accept an economic return on their investment. These folks are welcome to think of managing Global Warming as a side benefit… or as irrelevant – if their main or only goal is to simply earn a profit from their invested capital.

We've considered the economic opportunity from this system. But we need to consider two more key points. **First**, the backside of the second mirror blocks sunlight from reaching the Earth. Since sunlight reaches the entire area of both mirrors, but only one is sending solar energy to the other, the whole system reduces global warming when it is maintained inside the LP1 circle. **Second**, if we ever get into a situation where the Earth's temperature is becoming too cold – a new ice age – the ion engines can maintain the whole structure on a plane perpendicular to the Sun/Earth axial line and including LP1, but far enough outside of the LP1 circle so that it is now redirecting sunlight to the Earth that would otherwise have missed the Earth. Due to the geometry of the situation, only a small but continuously applied force is needed to permanently maintain such a position. Thus, by positioning the giant tethered mirrors either near LP1, where they redirect sunlight already heading for Earth, or off to the side far enough to redirect sunlight that would have otherwise missed the Earth, the entire system, with thousands or millions of tethered pairs of mirrors, functions as a giant Earth Thermostat – literally setting the temperature of the entire planet.

Other benefits can result from this system – including an entirely new science of weather management. Since weather is a function of air pressure, it should be possible to develop computer models that can direct solar energy in a way to produce situations of either low winds, or steady and continuous wind when this is desired for generating wind energy.

Developing a system to break up hurricanes before they form, or during the early stages of formation, should also be possible.

Since Dr. Angel published his 2006 paper, there has been a remarkable drop in the cost of chemical rocket launches. The single biggest factor is the innovation of reusable first stages. Imagine how expensive air travel would be if you had to use a brand-new airplane for each flight! Elon Musk has said reusable first stages will make it possible to reduce launch costs by up two orders of magnitude – a penny on the dollar. Thus, it is now becoming economically practical to launch commodities into space. Launching millions of tons of space-based mirror material, and assembling mirror structures in space, is now a practical option for humankind to consider.

Managing solar radiation reaching the Earth by building and maintaining what you could call "space pyramids" at LP1 is probably humankind's greatest political, environmental, and economic opportunity today.

The Public Utility part of Utility Solar Energy

The basic idea behind Public Utilities has already been covered in Chapter 3 -- we don't need to repeat it.

The only point to be noted here is that beyond a start-up phase, electric power from the whole system will be supplied on a cost-plus basis. That's the key.

Chapter wrap-up

As we've seen, there is tremendous potential for using giant mirrors in space to redirect sunlight in useful ways. We've also noted the impact this can have on Global Warming. As we've seen, by placing a combination of positionable tethered mirror pairs and surfaces to block sunlight at LP1, it's possible to build a giant "Earth Thermostat," allowing us to set the temperature of the planet. When we are using sunlight from orbiting mirrors, we need to keep in mind that in many and possibly all cases, the redirected sunlight would otherwise have missed the Earth. This must be compensated for by installing positionable and manageable sunlight blocking surface area at LP1.

7 – MY STATE BUDGET PERSPECTIVE

Minnesota's most recent budget forecast shows a $7.7 billion surplus. Below is a commentary article I submitted to the Star Tribune – they haven't published it (yet) but it was revised multiple times as I followed the debate. It sums up my overall approach and my year-end view – but some additional comment will be added at the end of this chapter.

Danger lurks: Minnesota's inflated surplus

by: Bob "Again" Carney Jr.

Stereotypical battle lines are already forming in response to Minnesota's $7.7 Billion budget surplus forecast. Democrats call for an expansion of Government. Republicans demand tax cuts.

The Star Tribune Editorial Board ("EB") is rightly disposed to recommend compromise and cooperation in proceeding (How to handle a massive surplus, Dec 11.) Unfortunately, the EB also advanced this flawed and dangerous assessment: "In another departure from previous surpluses, much of this one is made up of ongoing funds rather than one-time windfalls."

More recently former State Finance Commissioner Peter Hutchinson weighed in: suggesting the entire amount is available for new initiatives. Trust us! – safeguards would include some kind of recycled Social Security Lockbox -- and a Constitutionally dubious plan to administer it by using only high-tech angels. Count James Madison as skeptical.

Most recently the EB has suggested paring up two priorities – each involving $1 billion. Enhanced "Hero pay" would go to essential workers who bore the brunt and assumed the greatest risk during COVID. The State would also pay off the $1 billion deficit in our Unemployment Insurance ("UI") financing; it's now clear the Federal Government won't do this.

The EB's $2 billion pairing plan is significant progress because it would be one-time rather than ongoing spending.

This brings us to confront a reality that has been missed by everyone. Both Minnesota's economy and our budget are being brutally assulted by inflation. We're not looking at trouble with some cute, cuddly "Trillion Tribble" Star Trek surplus. We're looking at Minnesota's bruised and swollen economic muscle.

To understand how and why danger lurks in our inflation-swollen forecast, let's first look more closely at the forecast itself. Then let's contrast permanent solutions like new programs or tax cuts with a one-time "Inflation Tax Refund."

By design, our State budgets ignore inflation. Thus, the forecast's spending side was frozen when the Legislature adjourned (it fluctuates slightly.) But inflation doesn't ignore us, does it?! Because the real-time income side projects ever-more-inflated dollars coming in, it's up a little over $5 Billion. Inflation also impacted a shift of $3 Billion of revenue from the last to the current biennium. Add those two together and we're up over $8 Billion – down to $7.7 Billion due to a required contribution to Minnesota's "rainy day" fund.

From a practical economic viewpoint inflation and taxation are identical in this way: they both take away part of your personal spending power.

What has Minnesota's "inflation tax increase" been over the last year? Here's a simple, rough-and-ready ballpark answer: Inflation for the most recent year was 6.8%. Average annual inflation for the last ten years was

2.44%. Let's round (6.8% - 2.44%) down to a 4% Minnesota inflation tax increase, applied to Minnesota's economy. This is $374 Billion x .04 = about $15 Billion dollars.

Goodbye surplus! We've already "paid more" in lost spending power.

Minnesota should do three things. First, we should implement the EB's plan to pair $1 billion in "Hero pay" with $1 billion to pay off the UI deficit. This segues into a larger Point Two. At least in the short term, we need to think of even year Legislative sessions not as "bonding sessions" but as "Inflation Reality Check" sessions. As just one example of possible rethinking: Should we pay cash for capital projects in 2022? Why sell bonds to be paid back at high, inflation-driven interest?

Point Three: we should plan on refunding much of what's left with something like "Jesse checks" – an across the board "Inflation Tax Refund" for all Minnesotans. It's vital to compare tax refunds with tax cuts. A tax refund is a onetime event – something you get when you overpaid. Overwithholding from your paycheck is the classic example. Tax cuts are entirely different – they are permanent reductions, not onetime adjustments.

Returning now to the EB's earlier claim that this surplus different because it's "made up of ongoing funds rather than one-time windfalls" – it is true that the process of collecting revenue is on-going. But here's the danger: when (if?) inflation does subside, both sides of such a "compromise" approach -- half new government programs and half tax cuts -- will contribute equally to future structural deficits.

To summarize: while the EB has partially backtracked with their $2 billion pairing plan, many Democrats, many Republicans, and Mr. Hutchinson all make the same dangerous mistake in suggesting permanent responses – either new programs or tax cuts -- to our hopefully temporary inflation-driven tax overpayment challenge.

I'll offer up some elaboration on this. Many have criticized former Gov. Tim Pawlenty for refusing to allow tax increases, and for big State deficits, sometimes precipitating financial gimmicks. Here's the big picture that always got missed – I distinctly remember the news release from the Governor's office that pointed it out. For forty years before Gov. Pawlenty took office, the average *annual* increase in our state's budget was 10%. The word annual needs to be emphasized – because we have two-year budgets, this means the average budget cycle was increasing at over 20%. During his eight years, Gov. Pawlenty's track record was a downward shift to annual increases of about 3%. I've long said both that this was an over-correction, but also that a dramatic downshift from 10% a year increases *was* necessary. It was without question painful. There *were* large budget deficits, and accounting gimmicks *were* used. But Gov. Pawlenty's achievement: changing our base line from 10% a year increases to 3% a year increases, makes him unquestionably the most impactful of Minnesota's Governors over the last fifty years. Gov. Mark Dayton's budgets averaged closer to his predecessor Gov. Pawlenty's 3% annual increases than to the 10% annual increases of the 40 years before Gov. Pawlenty. Our current Gov. Walz's first budget was closer to the 3% annual increase benchmark; in my view this is due in large part to Republican control of the State Senate.

In recent decades Minnesota voters have preferred divided government: From 1980 to 2020 there was one-party (the DFL) control of both houses and the Governor's office for only two years. I am convinced that a Republican voice in the non-judicial branches of State government, together with the painful but necessary downshift that is Gov. Pawlenty's legacy, has made Minnesota's economy more productive and more competitive. We are all better off for it.

Thus, my focus as Governor will be on continuing a policy of ensuring that Minnesota's budget does not grow faster than our increasing population and our real productivity (economic growth adjusted for inflation) can support. This is my top fiscal priority. I'm not making any no-new-taxes pledge… but just saying: we need to be mindful of this sobering and educational history.

To this I will only add that I'm open to a discussion of how Minnesota's state budget can be leveraged to promote my **DO GET USE** agenda — but *only* if it can be done in a way that is both bi-partisan, and that does not involve a commitment to any significant *on-going* state spending. Any economic participation by the state must be structured in a way to guarantee that the state can only participate as a secured investor. Having said that, I'll also point out that there are enormous potential benefits from establishing Minnesota as business hub for the kind of initiatives I'm proposing — which must be rooted in the use of Public Benefit Corporations, and which must look primarily to how government can *get out of the way* as much as possible.

8 – MY PLAN TO GOVERN (IF ELECTED) AND TO IMPLEMENT **DO GET USE**

I'm *both* a Republican – and a republican… self-described as being from "the republican wing of the Republican Party." Of course, this phrase is inspired by Sen. Paul Wellstone, who said he was from "the Democratic wing of the Democratic Party." Wellstone's phrase is widely understood to be a swipe at the "Wall Street Wing" -- ascendent under President Clinton and the "New Democrats." Permit me to suggest that President Clinton's "new-New Deal" really amounted to this offer to Wall Street and big business: "Contribute to 'New Democrats' and you can finally have your dream – 'one party for the price of two.'" This is the situation I think we've be in until the 2020 election – when Sens. Bernie Sanders and Elizabeth Warren shook things up before succumbing to COVID and Bidenzzzzz. More recently it's emerged that the "woke Left" is more dominant in the Democratic Party and the Biden Administration than

Republicans were led to believe – judging by their bi-partisanship pitch in 2020.

The lower case "r" is not redundant and not a typo! Today everyone seems to be stuck somewhere between a "Policy" and a "Tribal" mentality – the process of government has been lost sight of. It's especially sad to me to watch "big R" Republicans lead the charge on this.

Let's back off from this Policy/Tribal tilt in our thinking, and review briefly the basic ideas behind a small-r "republican" form of government. A good starting point is to reflect on the fact that the word "guarantee" is used only once in our unamended federal Constitution. Here it is… Article IV Section 4:

"The United States shall guarantee to every State in this Union a Republican Form of Government, and shall protect each of them against Invasion; and on Application of the Legislature, or of the Executive (when the Legislature cannot be convened) against domestic Violence."

By and large our founding generation had a dim, wary view of human nature. Many people of that time saw humankind as fallen -- beset by original sin and temptation. They ("we" of that time) were also acutely aware of how differing beliefs could and did lead to violence: the history of Europe from the Protestant

Reformation forward was soaked in blood… and of course many came to the "new world" to escape religious persecution.

This wary world view is at the root of our republican form of government, which features three branches of government, the Executive, the Legislative and the Judicial, and which is also founded on an understanding that there must be a kind of "zone of liberty" for the individual – protection of each person's rights. Five core rights… sometimes called the "five freedoms" -- are provided for in our Constitution's First Amendment: speech, religion, the press, peaceable assembly, and petitioning the government for "a redress of grievances." Although there is little federal case law on the meaning of Article IV Section 4, it's fair to assume at a minimum that the three basic branches of government, and a written Constitution addressing the question of rights, are minimum requirements for any State.

This is the small-r view – and at least until recently I think it's been widely shared. But I also see it as under attack and breaking down. Partisans on both sides seem to be looking at each piece of the "machinery of government" as just another lever of power: something to be seized and controlled as a way of advancing a Policy/Tribal agenda.

My approach to serving as Governor is rooted both in the small-r conception of a "republican form of government" and an awareness of the deep divisions we have in American society today.

More specifically, beyond the confines of my **DO GET USE** agenda (including an expansive scope for transportation and transit issues considered in Chapter 11,) I am reluctant to advance any personal policy agenda of any kind. I do not – emphatically do not – view the Governor as a kind of "third house of the legislature." Rather, I believe a Governor should strive mightily to work with both houses and all parties represented in the Legislature, to arrive at a state budget and state laws that are the result of dialogue and compromise. This is why beyond the **DO GET USE** domain, I am not prepared to make promises on any policy question. I'm willing to describe general inclinations and values in the context of our current divisions, but that's about it. I will add this however: I am prepared to use the veto power to ensure that State spending does not go above something like a 3% or 4% maximum increase in inflation-adjusted dollars -- constrained by real economic and population growth and what we can reasonably anticipate about inflation. However, *how* the Legislature arrives at such a budget is in my view primary up to them – I'll simply do what I can to help reach compromises.

Regarding the Executive branch more specifically, I think a major role of the Governor should be questioning whether what is being proposed, and what is now being done, is rooted in practical realities. We need a government that functions efficiently and effectively, and one that is not bloated. We've had what I see as an unfortunate tradition of bringing a new set of Commissioners with each new Administration. I favor both seeking out Commissioners who are committed to an efficient and effective administration of their department, and who are committed to faithfully carrying out the written mandates and clear intents of State laws. My ideal is to both seek out people who will *not* be expected to resign when a new Administration comes into office. **Disclosure**: in High School I was on the Washburn Debate team. During one of our tournaments I debated Jan Malcolm. She impressed me then, and I asked her out. While I haven't reviewed criticisms of her, and their may be legitimate issues, I've been favorably impressed by her since way back.

As a general approach I would plan to review the performance of current Commissioners, and ask people to stay if I conclude they fulfill what I've just described as a "small r" republican view of their office.

However, beyond this approach to the Executive Branch – I'm also a big-R Republican. For this reason I'm strongly inclined to support Republican nominees for the

Legislature across-the-board. Having both houses of the Minnesota Legislature controlled by Republicans is a priority of mine. But having said that, I will not hesitate to speak out whenever I think institutional control is suppressing legitimate debate and dialogue in the Legislature on budget and other issues. We must ensure the Committee system is working, and all points of view are being heard and considered.

Political Outsiders – The "Ventura phenomena"

Among our 50 states, Minnesota has had a real and close-to-unique experience, complete with world-wide publicity, of being governed by a political outsider. Jessie Ventura – a former business associated and partly a product of Donald Trump, served as our Governor from 1999 to 2002. The "political rap sheet" on Ventura was that he was a total political outsider. Not quite -- he did in fact have prior experience in elective office, serving a term as the Mayor of Brooklyn Park, MN. He was also a well-known talk radio personality, after his colorful Wrestling-as-Performance-Art and acting careers. In short, before his election Ventura was well and widely understood by Minnesotans. We should also note that there was a kind of bi-partisan, rallying-round effect once he was elected. There may have been elements of necessity and near-desperation in this. Be that as it may, with some exceptions Ventura's administration was staffed with a bi-partisan collection of people widely recognized as fully capable of doing their jobs. Whatever your view of it might be, the Ventura Administration was by no means any kind of a disaster. And this is crucially important: it did not represent an attack or challenge to the core ideas and structure behind a republican form of government. These are important aspects to keep in mind.

Using the Ventura administration as a benchmark, here's my first claim: In terms of qualifications, I have a better background than he did in terms of both education and wide ranging work experience. I am more knowledgeable about both the principles and workings of government than he was. If elected, I'm confident Minnesota's establishment would rally around me just as it did around Gov. Ventura – and that I could put together an Administration with appointees of comparable experience and qualifications to those of his administration. Please notice: I'm using the Ventura administration here as an explicitly *positive* benchmark – something that (by and large) both can be measured up to and should be measured up to.

Beyond the nuts-and-bolts aspect of government, Gov. Ventura tried with mixed results to carry out another role both during and beyond his term. In his own way Gov. Ventura's activity was similar to Upton Sinclair's broad-based "Dead Hands" series of books in this sense – it was an across-the-board critique of American institutions and American culture. I went with my 2010

Lt. Governor running mate, Bill McGaughey, to one of Gov. Ventura's book-signing for <u>DemoCRIPS and ReBLOODlicans: No More Gangs in Government</u>; I bought a copy, which he signed, and read it. Please note: I don't know what Gov. Ventura's actual involvement was in writing the book; but I suspect that Dick Russell, his "as-told-by" co-author, did all the work. Finally, we should note that Gov. Ventura was widely criticized for exploiting his office for personal gain – in effect "working two jobs" while he was Governor. That's addressed at the end of this chapter.

In seeking to carry out my role as Governor, I plan to do some unusual things. There will be more information on my web site detailing this, along with arguments that although highly unconventional, everything I'm planning to do is legal. There are two main aspects to this:

First, when inaugurated I will immediately transmit to the Senate President and the House Speaker a "declaration of inability." The effect of this is that the Lt. Governor immediately becomes responsible for discharging the powers and duties of the office. Here's what this means: I will have no day-to-day operational responsibilities. However, I will still *be* the Governor. I can also at any time issue another "declaration to the contrary" – that's language from the relevant state Statute… in which case I would immediately resume the ability and responsibility to discharge the powers and duties of the office.

There are some major advantages from carrying this plan. The biggest is that a fully competent, experienced, widely respected, trusted person can be selected to serve as Lt. Governor. For all practical purposes, on a day-to-day operational basis, they will be the Governor – they will be making decisions, issuing orders, appointing people, signing bills, and so forth – in short… doing everything a Governor does.

However, they will always have someone looking over their shoulder: Me. In effect I will have a kind of "super-veto power" over everything they do. If they start to act in a way that violates my vision of how the office should be carried out – just described above – I can bench 'em, grab a helmet and get in the game myself.

The consequence of this reality is that I will be, in effect, the Lt. Governor's supervisor. We will meet frequently, and at length, to talk about what's going on. I will give my own assessment – almost always deferring to the good judgment of the fully competent, experienced, widely respected, trusted person that I will have the honor and good fortune to serve with.

At the same time, during Legislative sessions, I'll be free to spend the bulk of my time working with individual Legislators and Committees, as a facilitator… helping them to analyze and discuss issues, identify the best among competing ideas, and ultimately reach compromises that will take the form of our State's budget and policy legislation.

I'll also be free to engage in both constructive political activity – including taking on former President Trump when and as needed – and working to establish and advance the Public Benefit Corporations (there will be more than one) needed to advance my **DO GET USE** agenda.

Of course an obvious question pops up: how are we going to recruit the "fully competent, experienced, widely respected, trusted person" to serve as my Lt. Governor? If the GOP convention surprises everyone and endorses me this should not be a problem. However, I have a weird but legal backup plan for this too. Very simply, if I run in the GOP primary as an unendorsed candidate, I will recruit a Lt. Governor candidate who will promise, in writing and on video, that if we win the primary election, they will immediately leave the state and take up residence anywhere outside of Minnesota.

Here's why this weird step is needed: it's the only way to create a vacancy on the ballot for Lt. Governor. Unsurprisingly it is illegal for a Minnesota non-resident to be a candidate. According to State law, if someone is ineligible to serve in the office that they are seeking… they can be legally disqualified as a candidate, and they can then be replaced on the ballot.

This means that if I win the primary, we would then be in a situation where a replacement candidate for Lt. Governor could step forward. Naturally, I would be looking for someone who has already been described ad nauseum a: "fully competent, experienced, widely respected, trusted person." Such a person might be a person I defeated in the GOP primary. It could also be someone else who competed for the GOP endorsement but did not win it and did not run in the primary. In general it would be a person who fits the description I've offered.

One final point: suppose the person I ran with in the primary broke their promise and did not make themself ineligible to continue as a candidate. Their prior written and on-video pledge could include acknowledging that they could be and should be impeached if they were to do such a thing. However, here's an amazing bug: our State's Constitution does *not* enumerate the Lt. Governor as being subject to impeachment powers of the Legislature. Everyone else is listed… everyone else can be impeached. At this point, I'm not sure what to think about this… It's possible that if I issue my "declaration of inability" then because the Lt. Gov. would assume the powers and duties of the Governor, they would then become *eligible* for impeachment. Presumably, after the state House impeached them, I could issue my declaration to the contrary – by that time they would be impeached and the case would be before the state Senate. Another back up plan would be for me to simply not issue a "declaration of inability" until we figured out how to get rid of an AWOL Lt. Gov. who would go back on the pledge that they had made. Of course, a final option would be for the people of Minnesota to refuse to elect a ticket for Governor that included such an AWOL Lt. Gov. candidate. Under such circumstances I personally might vote for someone else in the General Election, and encourage others to do so. At this point, let's just note that there's a bug here and leave it at that for now.

This brings us to the concluding topic.

What "second job" or "outside employment" activities can, and should, a Governor engage in?

Of course, Gov. Ventura broke some new ground for these issues. Let's start with brief comments on two examples

First, on June 14th 1999, about half a year after Gov. Ventura took office, the Minnesota Campaign Finance Board issued an advisory opinion finding that the activities of a non-profit organization, Ventura for Minnesota, Inc. ("VMI") in licensing certain rights and commercializing products such as an "Ventura Action Doll" with a replica campaign button on it did not make VMI a political committee; therefore VMI was not required to establish a political fund. Frankly, the fact situation seemed pretty murky, but this is one place to look for emerging guidance on the unique situation Gov. Ventura was presenting.

Second, on August 19, 1999 Ramsey County Judge Kathleen Gearin dismissed an action by environmental activist Leslie Davis, who had sought an order prohibiting Gov. Ventura from refereeing a Wrestling match, while wearing a business suit rather than a referee's uniform. It was reported Gov. Ventura had the potential to make over $1 milllion in royalties from this event; he was also reported be donating his fee to charity. The dismissal was on the issue of Mr. Davis' standing to sue. [**Disclosure**: in 2010 I sued Gov. Pawlenty's Administration, challenging his unallotment of the Minnesota Political Contribution Refund program as illegal, that case also came before Judge Gearin who ruled against me on statutory grounds; she also heard a second unallotment case that went forward to the MN Supreme Court on a Constitutional issue I did not raise, (Gov. Pawlenty's Administration had appealed) – the Supreme Court ultimately decided the case against the Pawlenty Administration based on the same statutory argument I had raised before Judge Gearin.] Ultimately Ventura did referee the event – I haven't tried to dig further to find out how much he made personally from it – if anything.

Here's the bottom line. On the one hand, Gov. Ventura has established some precedents demonstrating that Governors **can** do what amounts to "holding a second job." More generally, what I'm proposing going forward has another new element – the use of the Public Benefit corporate form –only recently established by law .

At this point I'm planning things out in a way that will allow for me to have significant time to advance my **DO GET USE** agenda as legal outside activity while I am serving as Governor (if elected.) I will be transparent in disclosing what I'm doing and planning to do. Let me emphasize that my goal is to seek ways of serving the public government through what amounts to voluntary, private activity; I believe the Government's main and vital task in the long run is simply to get out of the way and allow this to happen.

However, let me add this: in the short term I'm not adverse to all kinds of possible public-private partnership approaches to help launch the activities that I see as carrying out **DO GET USE**. This may involve state money – and lots of it. I'd love to see public-private-partnership initiatives establish Minnesota as a world-wide hub for new business initiatives and entire new industrial sectors. But these are many bridges yet to be built… let alone reached… let alone crossed. As events unfold, we may need to have all kinds of new discussions. Right now I'm simply trying to broach and identify some of the issues that may be coming up. Of course, if you don't like how I'm thinking – don't vote for me!

9 – ANNUAL ELECTIONS CAN REVITALIZE OUR URBAN CORES – BOTH REPUBLICANS AND RANKED CHOICE VOTING ARE NEEDED

Last year I launched and ran what I thought was a productive campaign for Mayor of Minneapolis. Spending only $654 including the $500 filing fee, I received over 8,000 votes when you count all rankings (1st, 2nd and 3rd.) Below is my commentary article, published July 21st by the Star Tribune. Below that is my plan for advancing this idea further as your Governor.

Minneapolis needs annual municipal elections

By: Bob "Again" Carney Jr.

We've heard a lot lately about Republican voter suppression. Here's the generic charge: Suppression is directed against people of color and marginalized groups;

Republicans benefit because these groups tend to support Democrats.

But de facto voter suppression is arguably going on in many big cities dominated by Democrats — including Minneapolis.

How? Simple — they just don't hold many elections.

Minneapolis holds no election in three out of every four years. And unlike the alleged Republican voter suppression, the Minneapolis system works perfectly — 100% of eligible voters are suppressed in every non-election year.

Of course, every fourth year — like this year, incidentally — we still have one. But judging from the shortage of lawn signs, you'd never guess.

A big part of the problem is that the Republican Party in Minneapolis is dead. To illustrate, at my 2020 Republican precinct caucus I was able to push through to passage a resolution calling for then-President Donald Trump's second impeachment. Yea! The system works!

Here's the bad news: The vote was 1-0. I was the only Republican who showed up.

What's more, even when Minneapolis does (yawn) have an election, it's during an off-off year — the year before the midterm "off-year" election. Here's the history of turnout among registered voters in the last three city elections: 2009, 20%; 2013, 34%; 2017, 44%. [Note: the 2021 turnout was 54% -- obviously that wasn't known when this article was published.]

By contrast, in 2020, a presidential election year, Minneapolis voter turnout was 87%.

The city's de facto one-party monopoly, combined with one off-off year election every four years constitutes an across-the-board voter suppression system that really works. Republicans, who are dazed, canceled, wandering, astray and untethered from the very meaning of their party's name need to challenge this structural voter suppression Minneapolis has achieved.

In recent decades, no Republican has been anything but a curiosity in a Minneapolis mayoral election.

Two things are needed. First, we must have annual municipal elections in Minneapolis for at least the next 10 years.

The tradition of two-year terms for both the U.S. House and the lower chambers of all state legislatures is foundational to our system of government. But during the Revolutionary War period, even that hadn't been thought good enough. Many colonial assemblies faced voters annually. It's far too easy in the Minneapolis political environment for media, money and special interests to dominate the City Council and the mayor's office.

But if Minneapolis voters and officeholders came to understand that any elected official could be thrown out in less than a year, our situation could improve dramatically. People might also be more willing to try new ideas and new kinds of candidates if they knew election bestowed only a one-year warranty.

Second, the Republican Party must again become competitive in Minneapolis and St. Paul. We Republicans must welcome a range of people and ideas. The alternative is increasing trauma and instability in our political system.

And yes, things can get worse.

I'll be filing as a candidate for mayor, as a Republican — and hoping others do the same. With health issues and realizing my own limitations, I don't want to be mayor. My intent is to expose and challenge the status quo, and to offer a menu of possible solutions.

My promise is this: if elected, I'll resign before Aug. 9, 2022. According to law, that's the last date for the City Council to call a special election for a mayoral vacancy on the same day as the 2022 Minnesota general election.

I'll also lobby at the Legislature for annual Minneapolis municipal elections.

This is political trust busting. We need to break up the structural political monopoly in Minneapolis.

A lot of Minneapolitans are looking for new ideas this year.

As you can see from the note inserted in the article, turnout did rise to 54% -- continuing an upward trend line that I see as correlating with an increase in people who perceive major problems with our municipal government. But that's still over 33% lower than the 87% of Minneapolis voters who turned out for the 2020 Presidential election.

The biggest driver of last year's turnout was the so-called "defund the Police" City Charter Amendment. With crime and public safety now the number one concern of people in Minneapolis, that measure, which I strongly opposed, was defeated 56% to 44%.

But both the need and the opportunity for holding annual elections remains – and this is as much a potential opportunity for the whole spectrum of Democratic and Socialist candidates as it is for independents and moderates -- including Republicans.

As I claim in the article, the remedy for this de facto voter suppression really is "political trustbusting." And equally important, it's an opportunity for candidates to continually refine and improve their ideas – something I've personally been doing for over twelve years now – starting with my first candidacy for public office in the 2009

Minneapolis Mayoral election. Over those years, without any significant campaign spending, but with regular Star Tribune political opinion pieces, I've established a reputation – a brand ("Again") – and a wide readership. People have been and are listening to my ideas, which, I humbly submit, have been continuously improving.

Politics can be and should be a marketplace for ideas. But markets don't work if they're not open! Opening our urban core city markets for political ideas only one day out of every four years just doesn't cut it.

I want to offer up three further points here before wrapping up this chapter.

• First, annual elections… and yes, a kind of "permanent campaigning" – offers an opportunity to significantly reduce the control of money over politics. Especially at the level of Ward politics (Minneapolis has about 20,700 registered voters per Ward) a combination of canvassing, social media, and putting up letter and business card signs and messages on things like telephone poles, can get out the word about the ideas and proposals anyone is advancing, while requiring a bare minimum of money.

• Second, this shouldn't be regarded as a burden to currently elected officials. They can maintain their own campaign organizations, getting out their own message. With their built-in advantage of incumbency they can and should build and publicize their own reputation and track record – standing for election each fall.

- Third, this system will have the effect of linking national and local issues during Presidential election years, and state and local issues during mid-term general elections, when all State offices (sometimes excepting the state Senate) are up for election.

A Chapter-ending digression – making our state government more accountable

You can skip this and go to the next chapter… unless you're a nerd like me. Nerds of the world arise!... we have nothing to lose but our bookmarks. It's about 550 more words.

In Minnesota we have a kind-of-screwy system for electing state Senators. The term is declared to be four years. However, the current interpretation of our Federal Constitution requires an election after the redistricting that follows each census. As one way to comply with this requirement our state Constitution currently requires a new round of state Senate elections for every year that ends in "2" -- every XXX2. But because the term is declared to be four years, this means there will always three terms in a decade, including one that is only two years. Here's how this works: After the XXX2, the next term ends in XXX6, and the term after that ends in XXX0. Then the Census is conducted, and the pattern repeats: XXX2, XXX6, XXX0.

Let's consider an alternative approach that also complies with our current interpretation of the Federal

Constitution, starting with this fact: We have a census on odd decades every twenty years, i.e., 20_3_0, 20_5_0, 20_7_0, and so on.   Suppose that instead of our current system we require a "redistricting" state Senate election after each odd decade census… followed by another state Senate election in two years. Then the prevailing pattern of four-year terms would resume. Here's how this would work, with the "redistricting" election years underlined and bold: 2022, 2026, 2030, **2032**, 2034, 2038, 2042, 2046, 2050, **2052**, 2054, 2058, 2062, 2066, 2070, **2072**, 2074, 2078, 2082… and so on. Notice that for each even census decade – 2040, 2060, and 2080 -- the prevailing sequence of four-year terms ensures that a new state Senate is elected following each census, as required. Notice also that while this amounts to inserting only one additional election every twenty years, unlike our current system the result is not ten-year cycles with one two-year term followed by two four-year terms, but twenty-year cycles with two consecutive two-year terms once every twenty years. Things still add up: with two two-year terms and four four-year terms; (2 x 2) + (4 x 4) = 20. As with our current system, we still have six State Senate elections every 20 years.

Now (finally!) we can consider the advantage of doing this. Unlike our current system, we will always have a state Senate election when the Governor and the other state Executive branch offices are up for election. This is a way of ensuring that the policy direction of our state – as represented by all elected office holders (let's call them the "temp workers") of the two policy-making branches -- will be up for review every four years… or five times every twenty years. With our current system, the entire policy direction of the state is only on the ballot three times every twenty years – the three mid-term elections following every Presidential election year with "0" as the last digit. For the other two four-year Gubernatorial cycles in this twenty-year period we elect our state Senators when the Presidential election is held. Because the Governor and other Executive branch officers are not on the ballot for those years, we can't hold all state policy making elected office-holders accountable in any single election during alternating decades. In short, our current system makes our state Government less accountable to us.

I believe this would be a good change… so I'm proposing we amend our state Constitution to carry it out. What do you think?

10 – THE SCHOOL BUS DRIVER CRISIS – AND MORE GENERALLY OUR TRANSIT CHALLENGE

When I reached age 65 in the fall of 2018 I became covered by Medicare (so employer-paid health insurance wasn't an issue) but also in need of ongoing income. I was also looking for something to do that did not involve paying me to think – i.e. something that would let me think about the kinds of things that have led to this book during working hours. The things I had done before – typically computer programming and accounting/business projects, didn't meet that criteria (the puzzles that come with that type of work are things that keep my brain whirling when I'm off the clock.) So… I became a School Bus driver -- and have greatly enjoyed it. Due to a medical issue I'm currently unable to drive until February 2022, but plan to resume then. In the past few months I've been doing School Bus driver recruiting.

This new occupation also dovetailed nicely with my more general interest in transit. From about 2013 forward I hadn't driven a car – relying on public transit, walking, biking and sometimes catching a ride. That was an interesting education in itself. On the one hand I saw great potential for public transit; but I also saw that as a system it is woefully inadequate. After George Floyd's death – police officer Derek Chauvin was later convicted of murdering him in a jury trial -- I drove food delivery runs through the post-rioting devastation along Lake Street in South Minneapolis during the Summer of 2020. More recently some of my routes circled around 38th and Chicago, where he was killed. That was a major bus route intersection but has been occupied and closed off. During the 2019-20 school year it was on one of my routes, I drove by Chicago along 38th Street twice day.

One of my significant personal deficiencies as a School Bus driver is that I simply refuse to yell at people. Frankly, in some situations this is expected if not required – students can and do get out control. My company's management knows how I am; they assigned me to routes – sometimes "milk runs" – with students they knew I could manage without yelling at them… after all, those routes need drivers too. On one of my more challenging North Minneapolis routes I once heard elementary school students discussing the important difference between "tattling" and "snitching." Tattling is "telling on someone" at school – the students decided that was ok. They also decided that "tattling" is *different* from "snitching" – telling the police about something in a gang-infested neighborhood, is *entirely different*. These elementary students knew that "snitching" can result in someone being killed. They might be killed. Sadly this is part of the reality of their lives. Another time, just before the verdict in the Derek Chauvin trial, several thousand National Guard troops had been deployed as a precaution. As I was passing a pulled-over armored vehicle with a mounted machine gun and armed men, an elementary student asked me: "Are soldiers policemen now?" One of our drivers, who had students on board, once reported over the radio that an adult who had been shot had just boarded his bus… he was taking them to the nearest fire station. Once when driving I heard a loud "bang" ahead of the bus – a student asked me if I'd heard it and I said "yes." The student thought it was a gunshot and told me "I hear that a lot." I backed up quickly through one intersection and turned on to the cross-street. [Based on subsequent discussion, the sound I heard could have been a transformer blowing out – since the merger that formed Xcel Energy they no longer do preventative maintenance.]

This is all part of what is going on in our society today… part of my own education -- and obviously something that cries out for a remedy.

However, while the problems described above are real, they aren't the whole story. It's too easy for all of us to become absorbed with the 1% of anything that's bad… and lose sight of the 99% that's "meh" or above. By and large I've really been enjoying bus driving. I like kids… and it's fun to hear them chattering away with their friends. A lot of high school students, and some younger ones, use bus time to read or catch up on other tasks – as do many who use public transit. Still… riding a school bus is inherently a kind of limbo… something like **The Transit Zone** – to use 18 point "TwyliteZone" type. Here's the point – looking forward there are all kinds of ways to improve everyone's experience with **The Transit Zone**. We need to consider how we can improve the experiences people have with public transit generally.

My 2013 campaign for Mayor of Minneapolis was centered around <u>Demand Transit Revolution</u>, a book length plan for drastically improving public transit in Minneapolis. There's a lot of information on my ideas for public transit on my web site.

I've also been active in opposing the Southwest Light Rail expansion of the Green Line – which will extend it from Downtown Minneapolis to Eden Prairie. Frankly, this is an ongoing disaster – the cost has exploded to something now approaching $3 billion. The original plan was to include 50% funding from the Federal government – unfortunately when the budget was frozen for Federal purposes the Federal share was under $1 billion – so it looks like State and local taxpayers (mostly Hennepin County) will be on the hook for at least $2 billion – maybe more – by the time everything is done.

On February 14th 2014 the Star Tribune published my alternative plan for transit in the Southwest corridor. Eight years later, I submitted a revised version of that article. Most of the text was from the original article. I had actually highlighted it in **TwyliteZone** type font – partly to document "I told you so! – and partly to emphasize that we really *are* in the **TwyliteZone** with this project. The editor didn't go with that approach, but here the revised version, including the TwyliteZone highlighting:

Editorial Counterpoint:

Pause -- and plan anew -- on Southwest light rail

By Bob "Again" Carney Jr. FEBRUARY 9, 2022

The Southwest light rail project is a disaster, 19th-century technology at 22nd-century prices. However, transit in the corridor still can, and should, be redesigned and greatly improved.

The key is to understand that the right of way can still be repurposed as a bus rapid transit (BRT) and small-vehicle route.

I laid out a plan for this eight years ago in a Star Tribune counterpoint. What follows is an updated version of that article.

Back in 2014 Republican legislators wanted an alternative. Minneapolis officials responded with a challenge, saying the lawmakers should offer up "… a BRT-only, no-rail transit system. Then we could have a real debate."

A "real debate" would still be welcome in 2022! But let's expand our scope to a comprehensive vision of what we can truly do with transit. Let's think and plan using our knowledge of current and emerging technology. Let's plan on the scale -- with the 100-year time frame and public-private coordination -- that founded our Minneapolis park system.

A Southwest light-rail alternative should be shaped by three future-focused considerations: vehicle size, service frequency and automated driving.

Let's use Metro Mobility-size vehicles -- 24 passengers and one lift, combined with existing SouthWest Transit BRT buses. These cost about $70,000 new, compared with $3 million per light-rail car.

The light-rail plan features about 200 weekday trips. My transit revolution alternative averages about 10 people per trip, but with about 2,400 trips a day.

Here's your obvious thought: "Bob, you're crazy! Economies of scale — it's a slam dunk — light rail is the way to go!"

Well, let me sit you down for a shocking fact: I ran the numbers for part-time drivers (we'll need almost 700) at $17 per hour. Even with about 10 times as many discrete daily trips, the $35 million annual operating cost is about the same as the Met Council's $32.7 million light-rail operating cost estimate.

Let's now consider the advantages of having 10 times as many discrete trips. The service frequency could be much higher — every five minutes or better. We could tailor express runs for speed, with specialty runs and door-to-door shuttles to bring people to a much finer grid of destinations. Over decades, we could tailor a small-vehicle system for both speed and access. We could also integrate school bus, Uber/Lyft and public transit into one system.

Automated driving is still coming. When it happens — when drivers become the equivalent of elevator operators — the cost per driver ($0) will become the same for a Metro Mobility-size bus and light rail. Which system do we want our children and grandchildren to have when the switch begins? That's the decision we're making today. Still!

This approach could include a later plan for small Midtown Greenway vehicles from a new Greenway/Lake Street transit station on Interstate 35W, to and from downtown using existing MNPass lanes that are guaranteed congestion-free.

Two key points going forward: First, we'll still use the right of way — but with small vehicles and BRT instead of light rail. Second — skip the tunnels! Leave the metal side in by the Grain Elevator Condos — but just yank the rest out, except for a culvert at the road to Cedar Lake. Don't risk destroying our lakes.

I agree with House Minority Leader Kurt Daudt and State Senate President David Osmek, and disagree with the Star Tribune Editorial Board ("Audit, but don't halt, Southwest light rail," Feb. 8). In the short term — a year or two — let's just stop the Southwest light rail project. We need to regroup.

I'm a Republican candidate for governor with some new (well, in this case, eight-year-old) ideas. But unlike the other GOP candidates I won't shut up about this reality: Trump is an insurrectionist and must never be allowed on a ballot again. This is why the GOP/Trump machinery is trying to cancel me.

Let's demand a transit revolution. Let's build for future generations, instead of rebuilding the past.

Bob "Again" Carney Jr., of Minneapolis, is a Republican candidate for governor.

In short, transit is an issue I know a lot about; my involvement has included thinking, writing, and hands-on experience.

Recently, with COVID, there is a huge, nationwide School Bus driver crisis. During my 2021 campaign for Mayor of Minneapolis, on September 22nd, 2021 the Star Tribune published a commentary article presenting my plan for dealing with our current crisis -- here it is:

Steering through crisis: A bus driver's plan

By: Bob "Again" Carney Jr.

Minneapolis and the whole metro area are challenged today by a school bus crisis. Not enough school bus drivers are currently licensed and driving. As a result, public, charter and private schools are unable to provide reliable bus transportation for students. Urgent action is needed.

As a candidate-journalist, in the great tradition of Upton Sinclair, I'm working as a school bus driver. However, while I see and hear the challenges daily, I haven't seen a basis for any kind of "Transit Jungle" expose.

The base from which my bus route originates currently has only about half of the drivers we had before COVID hit in early 2020. Everyone is doing all they can, but route scheduling often is too tight. I am constrained by both privacy and employment issues from elaborating with details. But when you add together the awful state of Minneapolis streets (construction roadblocks are everywhere), COVID concerns and the perception of a dangerous Minneapolis — well, current conditions are against us.

As for hiring new drivers, even someone with school bus driving experience requires a full training routine — three days of in-class instruction and 30 hours or more of behind-the-wheel training. There just aren't enough people in the pipeline to support an expectation that the conventional "ramping-up" process is going to resolve this crisis any time soon. Emergency action is clearly needed.

What might be most productive and practical in the short run?

First: Pay students to ride public transit. Currently, a lot of students have free Metro Transit passes, but this isn't enough. Eligible able-bodied students — starting at somewhere between seventh and ninth grade — should be able to sign an agreement accepting a cash payment of $2 per one-way school trip — that's $4 a day, or over $80 a month — payable on an independent contractor basis. As part of the deal students must agree to be removed from the school bus list.

As a result, many school bus stops would be eliminated — routes could be consolidated or canceled.

In reality, the public is currently paying for two buses for every student — a Metro Transit bus with available capacity, and a school bus seat on an assigned route. If we canceled the school bus for some students, the result would be a savings in the total number of school buses required — but there would be little if any corresponding increase in the number of Metro Transit buses needed. There would probably be a net savings in public cost.

Second: Immediately shut down all street construction projects that can be stopped without interfering with below-pavement infrastructure such as sewers. Our Minneapolis street system is in chaos today. This affects the ability of everyone to get around — things appear to have been planned so badly, if planned at all, that we simply must stop all construction activity that we can before winter hits.

Third: Buy hundreds (maybe 1,000) of 12- to 15-passenger vans and make them available to any Uber, Lyft or taxi driver with a track record working for their company who is willing to drive scheduled morning and/or afternoon school runs. Safety equipment (a stop arm with a flasher, 4-way and 8-way lights,) can be installed as needed and a streamlined training system can be designed and implemented.

Routes can be designed to prioritize safety — avoiding van stops on busy streets, which can be left for buses with experienced drivers to handle. Each van can have radios. Routes can be scheduled using the same system we use to schedule school bus routes — the existing dispatch system can be used to manage and modify routes that are running. Obviously, there is a capacity issue — but many buses are already running with 15 or fewer students. The current hourly pay for school bus drivers is something a lot of Uber and Lyft drivers are likely to find competitive, and they've already prescreened for flexible schedules.

Fourth: Allow some (maybe hundreds) of current Metro Mobility drivers and vans to be deployed to run school bus routes.

Fifth: Negotiate with the U.S. Postal Service and possibly other large entities to make their employees available as part-time van drivers.

Sixth: Negotiate with schools to have their staff, including teachers, provide van driving service. Vans can remain at or near the schools during the day — everyone could commute to the school as they normally do.

Seventh: Consider mobilizing the National Guard as van drivers.

The next step will be to integrate the use of these vans with all elements of our existing transit system. We actually have several transit-transportation systems: Metro Transit, the school bus system, Uber/Lyft/taxis, the Metro Mobility system (part of Metro Transit but functionally separate) — and let's not forget the biggest one: private vehicles. All of these elements can be redesigned to work together if we are determined not to let special and parochial interests stop us from achieving the integration that is possible.

The status quo is a prison of our own making. The key is to devise a workable system and then demand that all special interests yield to the overall public benefits it will provide.

Bob "Again" Carney Jr. is a Republican candidate for mayor of Minneapolis.

As your Governor I would be very interested in working with the Legislature, other levels of government, and the private sector, to plan and carry out a revised approach to the Southwest transit corridor similar to what I described in my 2014 article. The main change is that we now have a dedicated corridor in place – our requirement is simply to use the surface for metro mobility sized vehicles and vans rather than Light Rail train cars. There are huge problems with the tunnel currently being built north of Lake Street – a revised plan can simply eliminate the need for it – possibly with an accommodation for the road where going to and from Cedar Lake. Here's the bottom line – we don't need the problems with underground water that we've taken on with the current tunnel plan. Let's just stop that.

A revised and rethought plan can still happen: again involving both Public Private Partnerships and Public Benefit Corporations.

As needed perspective on our challenge, let me wrap up this chapter by offering up one graphic, with some concluding commentary – to illustrate the incredible "planned inefficiency" of our current approach to public transit.

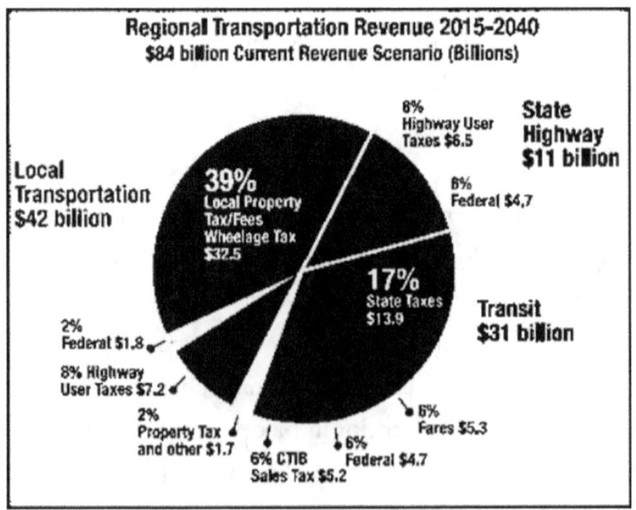

The pie chart on the last page is from Chapter 4 of the Metro Council's Thrive 2040 Transportation Policy Plan (Ver 1.0). Frankly, both the numbers and the general outlook & demeanor of this plan are pretty shocking. The chart is from the Current Revenue Scenario – defined as: "revenues that the region can reasonably expect to be available based on past experience and current laws and allocation formulas."

Let's stop and pick this data apart. Roads and Bridges is the necessary infrastructure for all non-rail travel – and cars are 98.6% of all travel (transit is 1.4%). But when we compare the spending, we find the 2040 Metro Council plan is to spend 37% of the total $(31/(31+42+11) = 37\%)$ on "transit". Since we're really concerned about money collected as taxes, let's back out fares: but even with that adjustment we're still spending $(31\text{-}5.3)/(31\text{-}5.3+53) = 33\%$ -- one third! – of *all* public dollars on "transit"… which yields 1.4% of all trips.

But wait… there's more! The Metro Council says the Current Revenue Scenario isn't enough. They say "need" an additional $7 billion to $9 billion in new revenue over 26-years – *above* the $31 billion already projected. This is what giant light rail boondoggles have brought us to.

Here's what I draw from this… and I've been saying it for years… going on a decade now: our current "plan" is *just plain crazy*. As noted, we're already running multiple, uncoordinated systems. Given that both Uber/Lyft and automated driving are coming on strong, we need to do some fundamental rethinking about both school bussing and public transit.

Here's one further factoid. We're all familiar with the sooty belch from school buses and other diesel big rigs. But a company called HyTech (for Hydrogen Technology) has a product on the market now that can inject a small quantity of hydrogen gas into each engine cylinder (called port injection) just before ignition. This greatly improves both fuel efficiency and reduces problems with the exhaust of these vehicles – so much so that diesel big rigs equipped with the HyTech system are reported to meet California's standard for low-emission vehicles. The improved fuel efficiency can sometimes cost-justify retrofitting diesel engines within months – not years. If this approach pans out, as HyTech claims it does, we don't need new and significantly more expensive electric busses, or natural gas powered buses. This is an example of **Green Energy Technology** – so it falls under the **GET** part of my overall **DO GET USE** plan – see Chapter 5.

To wrap up this chapter, we need a comprehensive rethinking of how we do school transportation, and public transportation more generally. Our focus going forward should be on providing well-paying jobs for people who drive – with minimum involvement of bureaucrats and support staff. That's another lesson I've learned from my current employer – everyone drives… from the company's President and the Base managers on down. This is **DO**

GET USE in action. We need to focus on the experience of using both public transportation and school transportation. We need to integrate school transportation with school more generally. When you enter any kind of school transportation, you are and should be in school — not in some weird Transit Zone.

What do you think?

11 – A CRITIQUE: UPTON SINCLAIR, SOCIALISM, POST-FDR, "CORPICA"; "PROGRESSIVE INSTITUTIONAL AUTHORITARIANISM;" SECULARISM; SIMULMATICS/BIG DATA AND VOTER MANIPULATION; THE "WOKE LEFT"

This is by far the longest chapter in the book. As you've seen, I have respect and regard for Upton Sinclair and his massive undertaking -- to analyze what I too see as a fabric-like American environment, carefully calculated to shape how we think and how we behave. I see the means of this shaping – maybe we should say there is a de facto control of all of us -- as having grown exponentially more powerful and more dominant since his writing and his 1934 campaign for Governor. As we'll see, while Sinclair was strongly opposed to how this means of thought and behavior shaping was being used, he was *not* opposed to its *existence* – only to the ends that he saw it serving.   In fact, it's clear that Sinclair both foresaw and favored its continuing development. For him, it was only a question of who would be in control.

It's here that we diverge fundamentally. As I see it, America has been increasingly shaped and controlled since before the "American Revolution" – which I've come to see more as America's first Civil War. My own perception is that from the Progressive era forward, America has become dominated what I call a "Corpica" regime of Progressive Institutional Authoritarianism. This has dominated not just both political parties, but the entire fabric of our country. Still… amidst all this I remain a small "r" Republican.

But rather than go further here in presenting my own thinking, let's first examine Upton Sinclair's pre-1934 writing – starting with the entire first chapter from <u>Money Writes</u> – the last of his six "dead hand" series of books. This will give you not just a taste but a full meal of how he thought and wrote. That first chapter is titled: CHRYSOTROPISM. It follows, set off from the remainder of this book by horizontal lines, indenting and rendering, as all quotes in this chapter are indented, with a different font (Times Roman.) One paragraph is followed by an editor's note saying the paragraph will be referred to later with a focus on the last portion… a little more than one sentence that I've highlighted in bold. Here we go.

Seventeen years ago I visited the marine biological laboratory of the University of California, and one of the world's greatest scientists explained to me his efforts at artificial fertilization. It was Jacques Loeb's thesis that all life is a chemical reaction; and to illustrate, he would take you to a little aquarium in which were swimming a number of tiny black creatures, the larvae of the sea urchin. The scientist would take a vial of salts and pour a few drops into the water, and instantly all the creatures would turn as one and swim towards the light. "That," said Loeb, "is what we call a 'tropism,' an impulse to move in a certain direction. In this case it is a 'heliotropism,' an impulse to move towards light. If we could enter the minds of these creatures, we should find that each is experiencing an emotion, each thinks that some reason of an important personal nature impels him to behave as he does. But science knows what has happened, the chemistry of the creature's cells has been altered. Some day – and not so far off – we shall understand human tropisms in this way, and be able to change by chemical agents the thing we call human nature."

I am writing upon the fifteenth of January, 1927, by the shore of that same ocean where the great scientist ventured his prophecy. The waters of this ocean are witnessing a singular event. It has been a damp and chilly day, and I look out over the sea from my study window, and the sunlight is failing, and a cold fog drifting in. The temperature of the water is fifty-seven degrees; and having been in for a few minutes during the day, I know that these suffice. Yet a hundred and three human beings, men and women, have chosen this day and night for an attempt to swim from Catalina island to the mainland, a distance of twenty-two miles at its shortest. The best time in which such a swim can be made is fourteen hours; and the radio tells me that all but a few of the contestants are falling out, many with bad cases of cramp, a few in delirium. Some will be injured for life; it may happen that one or more will lose their lives. A singular tropism to have seized upon a swarm of human urchins!

The answer is known to all readers of newspapers. Our leading California millionaire, purveyor or chewing-gum to the human race, had the idea a few years back to purchase Catalina island and turn it into a pleasure resort. This millionaire, having made his money by advertising, understands that in our great play-nation the one industry which is advertised free of charge is sport; a swimming race across the channel will bring millions of dollars worth of publicity, and so he offers a prize of twenty-five thousand dollars [Ed: indexed to 2022 dollars this is about $400,000.] He might have the race in midsummer, when it would be a pleasure; but this would defeat his purpose – to promote to the world that from his island it is possible to go swimming in January. Therefore he sets this date, and pours a few drops of tincture of gold into the social aquarium, and a hundred and three human urchins, male and female, are seized by an impulse which Jacques Loeb would have called a "chrysotropism."

The arts of producing social tropisms have been enormously developed in modern civilization, but the developments are so recent that we do not realize them as yet. We are used to hearing about "mob emotions"; but the fact is, this stage of human life is gone forever. No longer is the public permitted to originate its own tropisms, and run wild; **the social mind now has masters. Shrewd gentlemen sit in swivel chairs and consult with subordinates as to what tropisms they desire to have created; and either these tropisms are created, or the masterful gentlemen find more competent subordinates.** [Ed: please make a mental note of this paragraph, especially the portion rendered in bold – it will be specifically referenced later.]

These artificially created tropisms constitute everything really significant in present-day life. "World's series" tropisms and prize fight tropisms, evangelistic tropisms and moving picture tropisms, chewing-gum and safety razor tropisms, Harding-

Coolidge tropisms, anti-German, anti-Russian, anti-Mexican tropisms – do you think I exaggerate in saying that such mass-emptions are now made to order, by means of so-and-so many gallons of tincture of gold? Consider, for example, the ancient national antipathies; it used to be the case that these emotions had vitality enough to run themselves; but look at the urchins of France, how completely they were possessed, ten years ago, by an anti-German tropism, and how this has given place to anti-American, anti-British, and anti-Italian tropisms! Any social chemist, knowing the formulas of the diplomatic tinctures, can explain to you that the French owners of iron have made a deal with the German owners of coal, and so have cancelled their orders for anti-German tropisms, and called instead for tropisms against American bankers and British oil concessionaires and Italian traders in Tunis.

I am dealing in this book with a group of human urchins who hold themselves haughtily above the influence of social chemicals, the tropisms which move the vulgar herd. These lofty ones are the artists; my own tribe, the men and women of letters, who sit perched upon the apex of sophistication, and look down with scorn upon all mass emotions. But observe the singular phenomenon – on approximately the same date several thousand men and women of letters retire to secluded corners to excogitate a thing described as "charm"; each cudgeling his or her head for some variety which can possibly be regarded as original; each delving into dusty tomes in libraries, looking up costumes and accessories, weapons, liquors and far-off, forgotten oaths; each sitting for hours a day pecking at a typewriter, with one eye on the clock and the other on the calendar. Finally, on a certain date, several thousand men and women emerge from seclusion, each one carrying a manuscript of approximately the same size, and the same general style and spirit.

Is this not obviously a tropism? And what has happened to cause it? A magazine or publishing house has poured some drops of tincture of gold into the literary aquarium, and several thousand book urchins have been seized by a simultaneous impulse to feel "romantic" and to put these feelings into a novel of from eighty to one hundred and fifty thousand words not later than May 1st, 1927. In what way are these competing book urchins different from the sea urchins battling the waves in front of my home tonight? I take up the local evening paper, and on the front page I find a cartoon, "Wonder What a Catalina Channel Swimmer Thinks About." There are six little pictures, showing a swimmer in six positions of agonized effort; above the head is a legend, in larger and larger type, as follows: "25,000 berries! 25,000 beans! 25,000 bones! 25,000 simoleons! 25,000 shekels! $25,000!

Wonder what the writer of a $25,000 prize romantic novel thinks about!

So there you have it — just one unexploded shell from a voluminous arsenal of ammunition Upton Sinclair had produced for his opponents to volley at him during his 1934 **EPIC** campaign for Governor.

To assess Upton Sinclair's views and accomplishments, let's start with two basic points. **First**, he was a writer — a polemicist and advocate. While I don't think his first chapter is a caricature, it is definitely an exaggeration. More specifically: human beings are *not* slimy squirmy little larvae. True… the choices we make *are* made in a highly conditioned environment — both our thoughts and our experience of the world are impacted by a constant bombardment of behavior-modifying techniques and technology.   But there is still an element of real choice — an ability to mentally identify at least two courses of action in a situation and to deliberately choose one of them. I don't think this will ever go away. At a minimum Upton Sinclair exaggerates.

Second, we should consider improvements in the circumstances of people in America -- circumstances that Upton Sinclair railed against throughout his career before his 1934 campaign. There was much change for the good during the post-FDR New Deal decades. And after all, Upton Sinclair himself *switched* to the Democratic party *because* of the potential he saw for making what he envisioned as real progress by aligning with the Democrats.

Upton Sinclair's new party led the way to our foundational Social Security system, and to a Federal-level safety net and Administrative state that have made America a fundamentally different country compared to what we were before the New Deal. FDR's tent was a big tent – Ronald Reagan started out as a New Deal Democrat. Unions (Reagan was once the President of *a* Union… before he was President of *the* Union) could and did use economic strikes, but not general strikes, to lead the way to better wages, benefits and working conditions – non-union companies had to improve to be competitive.

The New Deal became fully bi-partisan with the election of President Dwight Eisenhower in 1952. Our system of interstate highways was introduced during the Eisenhower Administration, making coast-to-coast travel and trucking far more economically efficient, and also improving safety with divided highways that prevented head-on collisions. The Civil Rights era was also beginning, with the Supreme Court's unanimous 1954 *Brown v Board of Education* case, overturning the "separate but equal" doctrine of *Plessy v Ferguson*. That led with "all deliberate speed" to the Civil Rights and Voting Rights legislation of the Johnson Administration – by the way, overwhelming Republican support for these bills in both houses of Congress was essential to passing it. Workplace safety has improved dramatically, also driven by Unions and leading to the Nixon-era Occupational Safety and Health Administration. The Environmental Protection Agency was another Nixon-era program – improving the quality of life for everyone. Both Medicare and Medicaid were established during the Johnson Administration, the Medicare drug benefit was added during the second Bush Administration. President Obama's Affordable Care Act has had a major impact in ensuring all Americans can have health care coverage – although some States still choose not to participate in the Medicaid expansion. The Americans With Disabilities Act, introduced during the first Bush Administration, expanded opportunities for Americans to work productively.

All of these advances can be traced to a fundamental change in the way Americans have come to see the role of government since the foundational New Deal. And while losing his election, Upton Sinclair contributed ideas, especially production for use, to FDR's broader New Deal program. Of course much of Upton Sinclair's earlier Socialist political base also made the switch to supporting FDR's New Deal.

Notice there is a bi-partisan pattern in the above survey of major changes. New initiatives and new programs began in *both* Democratic and Republican

Administrations. Presidents Eisenhower, Nixon and Reagan can all be seen as "New Deal Republicans" -- establishing an enduring and bi-partisan foundation that broadly continued and expanded the New Deal's approach – a more active government at all levels, featuring a social safety net. There were obvious changes – the biggest was backing off Johnson's Federal-centric "Great Society" approach, favoring a "New Federalism" and "Deregulation" approach advanced by Presidents Nixon and Reagan. And of course, the massive downward adjustment at the top end of federal tax rates under President Reagan was a central feature of his economic agenda. President Reagan -- who majored in Economics in college -- merits further special attention here regarding Social Security. This was and still is the centerpiece of the New Deal… the Alphabet Soup of newer and Johnson-era regulatory programs not so much. When President Reagan famously said: "I didn't leave the Democratic party, it left me." -- it was the "Alphabet Soup" Great Society party of President Johnson that drove President Reagan away, together with the rising counter-culture of the 60s and 70s – not the FDR/Social Security party. But consider this: during President Reagan's first term the financial foundation of Social Security… FDR's centerpiece… was in crisis -- immanently in danger of running out of money. President Reagan led the way to *rescue* Social Security – by establishing the Greenspan Commission, which fundamentally strengthened its financial foundation.

Greenspan's restructuring is still holding today – although another crisis looms.

President Reagan was also a Goldwater supporter in 1964, giving his famous "A Time For Choosing" speech. But let's consider the content of that speech. While warmly embracing Senator Goldwater personally, President Reagan also proclaimed the need for what became Social Security's Supplemental Security Income program – enacted during the Nixon Administration. While opposing President Johnson's Medicare program, Reagan also recognized the obligation to provide for basic health care for seniors. Here's the real deal on that speech: on the one hand President Reagan was warm and friendly to Senator Goldwater personally, and voiced a generalized opposition to the thrust of LBJ's "Alphabet Soup" Great Society agenda. But on the other hand President Reagan *also* staked out a series of economic positions that would result in Reaganomics becoming significantly closer to the overall themes of the New Deal than the agenda Senator Goldwater had promoted. To sum up: when President Reagan took the modern Conservative movement's mantle from Senator Goldwater he shaped the policies of that movement towards a kind of "Conservative Wing" of a continuing and bi-partisan New Deal in ways many people haven't fully realized. I think President Reagan's moderate (compared to Goldwater) economic positioning of the Republican party -- his recognition that yes... Government *does* have a significant stabilizing role in our economy -- is foundational to the political success Republicans enjoyed during the Reagan era. We should also acknowledge that much of this record was made possible by the unique position of economic hegemony the United States enjoyed in the decades after World War II, as the only country that emerged unscathed. We were not bombed or occupied.

However, there is also much to critique about the changes we've seen in the nearly one century since Upton Sinclair's 1934 campaign.

One aspect to consider is an across-the-board acceptance of the post-New Deal idea that Congress can delegate "technical decision-making authority" – which some argue becomes policy making authority on a de facto basis – to all kinds of entities, agencies, boards, commissions, etc. On its face, the idea that "we should let the experts handle it" makes general sense. But there is an inevitable loss of accountability built in to this process. This makes the actual functioning of government subject to all kinds of "pressure points" – and to de facto control by the process of who is appointed or otherwise put into positions as decision makers and authorities.

My biggest concern is with the social-conditioning-and-control theme that launched this chapter. Two post-1934 books are good expositions of the line of thinking represented by the above chapter from Upton Sinclair. Aldous Huxley's (a writer critiqued by Upton Sinclair) wrote <u>Brave New World</u> (1932) - a fictionalized dystopian illustration of what an "engineered" culture might look like centuries from now – when people would be incubated in test tubes and conditioned to become something like living robots. In 1940 the well-known Christian writer C.S. Lewis published <u>The Abolition of Man</u>, three essays derived from BBC broadcast lectures that amount to a kind of theoretical basis for the fictionalized <u>Brave New World</u>. Professor Lewis begins with the idea that "debunking" things is a pretty easy thing to do -- but if you concentrate on "debunking" everything, you can easily reach a point of losing sight of all values of any kind. Professor Lewis thought the emerging capacity to "engineer" people could become so powerful that one day a group of people could literally decide what all future people would be – how they would think and behave. He asked the question: how would such a group of "humankind engineers" be guided in their "new creating?" He concluded that the result would be the <u>Abolition of Man</u> in this sense: While men before the "engineer-conditioners" were guided by a common moral law woven into all cultures, there was no reason to think that the "engineer-conditioners" would be or *should be* guided by it. Ideas like "freedom" and "dignity" – or ideas having any root in any traditional religion – were, at best, a menu of available options for the "engineer-conditioners." Professor Lewis thought that when this elite group came to understand their situation, they would not see themselves as compelled, or even guided, by ways of thinking that they themselves knew how to produce… or *not* produce.

More recently this line of thinking may have surfaced most visibly and decisively America with the publication of behavioral psychologist B.F. Skinner's 1971 book <u>Beyond Freedom and Dignity</u>. Ultimately this seems to be a kind of cookbook for the thinking that Upton Sinclair advocated for: a kind of dominant "Progressive Institutional Authoritarianism" that I see as tracing back to… duh… the Progressive Era. It also seems clearly to represent a plan to go forward to produce the elite group of "engineer-conditioners" that Professor Lewis foresaw as he warned us about a void of value they would inevitably step into.

The thesis of <u>Beyond Freedom and Dignity</u> is that behavioral psychology presents us with an opportunity to reach a new and scientifically founded understanding of what both individual human beings are, and what human cultures are. Professor Skinner's focus is not on what people have been held to "think," or "believe," or "feel" – all in his view murky and unscientific concepts -- but rather on how human beings behave, and how behavior can be shaped and conditioned, if not controlled, by "designing" or "engineering" the environment we live in. Professor Skinner favored developing and continuously improving a "technology of behavior" that will enable humans to "engineer" cultures to increase their ability to survive. He sees the survival of a culture as a kind of ultimate "scientific" value – but scientific only in the sense that he thought it could be derived empirically, by observation. He also sees humankind as in danger of extinction if we do *not* develop and deploy an increasingly effective "technology of behavior."

Professor Skinner saw our traditional ideas about "freedom" and "dignity" as dangers, or threats, to the survival of humankind as a species – and thus as possibly the ultimate challenge to humankind's survival. He therefore advocated that we must in some way move "beyond" a kind of ideology centered on the concepts of "freedom" and "dignity." More specifically, he advocated modifying our culture's system of conditioning and behavior-inducing rewards to both promote humankind's survival, and to diminish and eventually eliminate the threat posed by the "ideology" of freedom and dignity. This is my best effort at a succinct rendering of his thinking.

To connect this with Upton Sinclair's thinking, let's hearken back to the introduction of this chapter, and to the highlighted phrase: **"the social mind now has masters. Shrewd gentlemen sit in swivel chairs and consult with subordinates as to what tropisms they desire to have created; and either these tropisms are created, or the masterful gentlemen find more competent subordinates."**

Professor Skinner envisions Upton Sinclair's "competent subordinates" of "masters" of the "social mind" (p 149-50) this way:

"… as we come to understand the relationships between behavior and the environment, we discover new ways of changing behavior. The outlines of a technology are already clear. An assignment is stated as behavior to be produced or modified, and relevant contingencies are then arranged. A programmed sequence of contingencies may be needed. The technology has been most successful where behavior can be fairly easily specified and where appropriate contingencies can be constructed – for example, in child care, schools, and the management of retardates and institutionalized psychotics. The same principles are being applied, however, in the preparation of instructional materials at all educational levels, in psychotherapy beyond simple management, in rehabilitation, in industrial management, in urban design, and in many other fields of human behavior. There are many varieties of 'behavior modification' and many different formulations, but they all agree on the essential point: behavior can be changed by changing the conditions of which it is a function."

While Professor Skinner explicitly doesn't accept Professor Lewis' perspective he at one point both comes to grips with past centuries, and seems to anticipate America's situation today… writing (p 164-65):

"It is sometimes said that the scientific design of a culture is impossible because man will simply not accept the fact that he can be controlled. Even if it could be proved that human behavior is fully determined, said Dostoevsky, a man 'will still do something out of sheer perversity – he would create destruction and chaos – just to gain his point… and if all this could in turn be analyzed and prevented by predicting that it would occur, the man would deliberately go mad to prove his point.' The implication is that he would then be out of control, as if madness were a special kind of freedom or as if the behavior of a psychotic could not be predicted or controlled.

"There is a sense in which Dostoevsky may be right. A literature of freedom may inspire a sufficiently fanatical opposition to controlling practices to generate a neurotic if not psychotic response. There are signs of emotional instability in those who have been deeply affected by the literature. We have no better indication of the plight of the traditional libertarian than the bitterness with which he discusses the possibility of a science and technology of behavior and their use in the intentional design of a culture."

It seems to me this attitude of "rebellion against being controlled" is the real heart of President Trump's base. We'll come back to this. But we should note first that Professor Skinner was strongly challenged when he launched <u>Beyond Freedom and Dignity</u>. A good example of this was a discussion between Professor Skinner and a Christian, Professor Donald MacKay, a scientist (physicist), moderated on William F. Buckley's "Firing Line" (enter "Buckley Skinner Firing Line" in the youtube search box.)

Before relating the development of the "social mind" -- from Upton Sinclair's vision of it, which points directly to Professor Skinner's approach, and leads us to our present "rebellion" of Trump's base -- let's consider one more major change: the development of what I call "Corpica." This is framed in a graphic, shown on the next

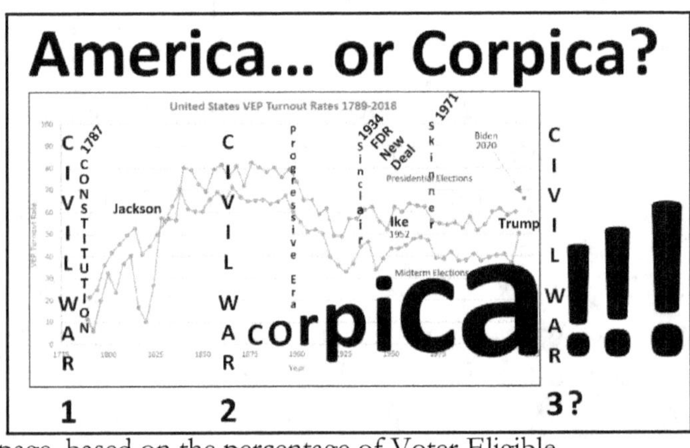

page, based on the percentage of Voter Eligible Participation ("VEP", see electproject.org) turnout throughout America's history as a country, featuring what I see as nothing short of the "replacement" of our traditional idea of "America" by "Corpica." By the way, VEP is of course based on eligible voters, something that has changed over time. By Andrew Jackson's presidency this meant most White adult males – since then Blacks,

Women, American Indians, and people age 18 or over have come to be included.   By the way… Disclosure: I believe I've coined the word "Corpica" for this reason: I own the domain name www.corpica.com. The fact it was unclaimed and available -- for ten bucks on GoDaddy… just a few months ago -- is frankly something that greatly surprised me.

Rather than burden you with a lot of detailed arguments (this chapter is already too long) let me just offer up some bullet points. I think I can support each one with convincing evidence… but won't try for now.

• The "American Revolution" is better understood as CIVIL WAR 1. We don't hear much in "history class" (Propaganda 101?) about the Tories… those LOSERS! – but there were a lot of them – and the fighting within many American communities was brutal… especially in and around Boston. Read <u>Tories</u>, (2010) by Thomas Allen for a detailed account.

• Democracy really took off in America with President Andrew Jackson – that's when the voter turnout percentages for Presidential and Midterm elections first crossed over – Presidential elections have become dominant. This led to a 60 year period from about 1840 to 1900 when Presidential VEP turnout (ignoring three "dip" elections) averaged about 80% -- roughly what we would expect based on the history of other "advanced" democracies around the world. The period up to CIVIL

WAR 2 (AKA *the* Civil War according to Conventional Wisdom) is one that I call "Party Chaos" – six different "parties" won the presidency; parties were often regional, not national; from 1828 to 1860 only one president (Jackson) was re-elected; and the Electoral College failed to elect a president twice – the only two times this has happened in our history.

•   From after CIVIL WAR 2 to the present we are in what I call the "two National Parties" period. During that time we have always elected a President from one of only two parties. Both parties are national, not regional – meaning that over multiple election cycles they both win significant percentages of voters in all geographic regions, and are able to elect Electors, Governors, State legislative majorities, and members of Congress from all geographical regions (the South has often been largely but not unconditionally an exception to this.)

•   Since we count seceded and unreconstructed States as having zero eligible voters, the VEP percentage remained stable right through CIVIL WAR 2, and up to about 1900. Blacks voted in large numbers immediately following CIVIL WAR 2 – but Southern Whites reestablished a position of power in the Democratic party – rooted in their ability to control and deliver a major block of Electoral votes -- and became able to effectively suppress Black voting. We then see what I call "the Big Slide." From the approximate start of the Progressive Era, to about 1920 – when Women started voting – the VEP percentage dropped dramatically for both Presidential and Mid-term elections – establishing new longterm baselines about 30% below the "Golden Age of Democracy" from 1840 to 1900. We'll come back to this.

•	The Progressive Era began with strong progressive constituencies in both parties. I think this led us to a situation where our two national parties tended more and more towards being two wings of a single "Corpica Party." While the two wings have contended for power, there has been a basic, continuing forward thrust towards an overarching, evolving and inexorably consolidating "Progressive Institutional Authoritarian" agenda.

•	The delegation of legislative authority to all manner of "bodies of experts," seen by some as a de facto delegation of policy, is a major aspect of Corpica. One big reason for this is that the career paths of individuals can zig-zag between employment by corporations and employment by all kinds of government entities. There can be an expectation of how people will behave as members of a "body of experts" based on both their employment history, and also based on the career paths that will be open to them if they assume and play a predictable role in some "body of experts." The phrase: "the regulated regulate the regulators" is explained by this "career path web."

This brings us to the main claim I'm offering up for your consideration in this chapter: the crucial rise and current total dominance of "Corpica" – a dominance that greatly facilitates the managing and manipulation of our behavior.

"Corpica" is defined empirically. The idea is not limited to for-profit business corporations. These may be the most important single form, but there are many corporate forms. To understand the full extent of Corpica let's simply list some major types of Corpica organizations.

• Most small and mid-sized businesses (some are partnerships and proprietorships)

• All non-profit corporations.

• All universities and colleges.

• All "bodies of experts" established, controlled, or regulated by some level of government.

• All private schools.

• All hospitals and nursing homes.

• All religious organizations – from the individual congregation level on up.

• All unions, including unions for educators and public sector unions.

• All trade and industry associations and organizations.

- All units of government below the State/County level, including cities of all sizes.

- Almost all news organizations.

Here's the point: if we look at "America" as a giant system for controlling human behavior, this control is carried out primarily by means of a web of Corpica organizations. In turn, as a group, these Corpica organizations control who runs our government(s) and how our government(s) control us.

The whole thrust of Upton Sinclair's critique in his six "Dead Hands" books was about how this control was exercised during his whole adult life, up to his run for Governor when his 50s.

Of course in the graphic I've included Skinner as one of the vertical name/event lines – right up there with Civil Wars, the Progressive Era and so forth. And just in terms not necessarily of a causal relation, but certainly of a correlative relation, it's striking to see how the Skinner line correlates to both a sudden drop, and a remarkably steady level, in Midterm VEP percentages. For forty years -- from 1974 to 2014 -- this Midterm VEP percentage was both at an historically low level, and showed almost no variance from cycle to cycle.

The People-Machine and the 1960 election

So far we've considered the power of media – from Upton Sinclair's <u>The Brass Check</u> forward – and the unrelenting march of applied behavioral psychology, from Upton Sinclair's portrayal of "people as sea urchins" responding to a tropism and moving in a single direction. But we haven't yet considered the revolutionary impact of computers, the internet, big data, and artificial intelligence. This whole technological ball of wax is another game changer. But its impact goes back to quite a bit before the PC Revolution triggered by Apple in the 1980s.

Early computers were coming into widespread use in America by the 1950s. In this chapter section, which is partly an extended book review, I'm relying heavily on a fascinating recent book, <u>If Then</u>, (2020) by Harvard historian Jill Lepore. It is the story of Simulmatics Inc., an early forerunner of the use of computers to simulate all kinds of aggregate human behavior, with an emphasis of how and why people vote, and how political campaigns can attempt to predict the results of their actions to shape both events and perceptions of events.

Although our chronology is fuzzy here – we've first considered B.F. Skinner's <u>Beyond Freedom and Dignity</u>, (1971) which came after Simulmatics had gone bankrupt – Skinner's book can be thought of a kind of "coming out party" for academic work and thinking that had been going on for a long time, and that was entwined with using computer technology to shape political campaigns since Adlai Stevenson.

This impact reached a turning point in the 1960 presidential campaign – when arguably the "People-Machine" that Simulmatics put to work for the Democratic party and the Kennedy campaign was decisive in winning the White House.

Fear of the impact of automation as a cause of job displacement goes back that far too. The 1960 Democratic platform had a plank laying out plans to help people who were losing jobs due to automation. Here's the cover of a 1960 Kennedy campaign brochure, addressing this issue explicitly by asking: "If automation takes your job… who will you want in the White House?"

The pitch then of course was that people matter – and that a particular person… Senator John F. Kennedy, should be there because he would be looking out for you.

But was Kennedy himself a puppet… or the product… of a machine? This emerged as a real question after the 1960 election. More specifically, a national media fire-storm and debate was triggered. By the way – you'll see the term "punch card." Some people might be unfamiliar with this. Punch cards were used in the early days of computing to enter information into a computer. They are similar to documents that are scanned today – but instead of coloring in bubbles with a black pen, small rectangles were punched out in patterns on the cards – the grid of punched-out rectangles was a coded form of the data to be entered. Let's pick up on this with an extended excerpt from Professor Lapore (page 126):

"The January 1961 issue of *Harper's* magazine hit newsstands the week before Christmas and stayed there nearly until Kennedy's inauguration. It featured a shocking story about how a top secret computer called 'the People-Machine,' invented by the 'What-If Men' of a magnificently mysterious organization known as the Simulmatics Corporation, had in effect elected Kennedy. Harold Lasswell announced, 'This is the A-bomb of the social sciences.'

"The *Harper's* story was picked up all over the country. It hung over the incoming administration like a storm cloud.

"The *New York Herald Tribune* reported that the People machine, 'a big, bulky monster called a 'Simulmatics,' had been Kennedy's 'secret weapon.' According to the Chicago Sun-Times, in the future, the directive of all politicians, before acting, would be to 'Clear it with the P.-M.' An

Oregon newspaper editorialized that, by way of Simulmatics, the Kennedy campaign had reduced 'the voters – you, me, Mrs. Jones next door, and Professor Smith at the university -- … to little holes in punch cards, or whatever device our new Ruler uses – and we were fed into the maw of the new Ruler and came out as the new standards to which we will ultimately conform, standards quite frankly called a 'model' of 'the public.' It described the tyranny of the People Machine as making 'the tyrannies of Hitler, Stalin and their forebears look like the inept fumbling of a village bully' because it contained no possibility of – and itself suppressed – the very idea of dissent.

"Most of the questions and concerns raised in the early decades of the twenty-first century about computers and politics were first raised in the 1960s, about Simulmatics' People Machine. Can computers rig elections? What does election prediction mean for democracy? What does automation mean for humanity? What happens to privacy in an age of data? Most of these questions had been asked in that very first story, in *Harper's*: 'If in a free society, information is power, how do we prevent tampering with the data provided by the machine? As we approach a consensus of opinion, what happens to freedom and spontaneity? As we seek more and more data for the machines, can we maintain our traditions of privacy?' The *Harper's* story didn't offer answers to those questions. Nor did the Great Brain of Behavioral Science, Harold Lasswell, who was quoted in the piece offering this particle of wisdom: 'You can't simulate the consequences of simulation.' The oracle had spoken.

Here's the brief author blurb inserted in the *Harper's* article by the editors:

"A free-lance writer whose work has appeared in many magazines, Thomas B. Morgan formerly was a senior editor of "Look" and features editor of "Esquire." His documentary film script on Albert Schweitzer won an Academy Award in 1957. A native of Springfield, Illinois, he was educated at Carleton College."

You might think: "how encouraging – that our reputable print-based media of that era were so willing to consider and debate important if controversial issues. And… Of Course… "Carleton College"… more Minnesota!" Some buckets of sobering, cold-water-in-your-face are called for… here they come.

News-Flash… er… Cold-Water-in-the-face-Splash One: you might wonder how Morgan knew so much about this "top secret" People Machine. The brief *Harper's* bio-blurb gives us some useful information – it was probably a memory-jogger for most of the magazine's readers – "oh yeah, that guy… I remember reading…" But as Professor Lapore points out, the blurb neglected to mention what would be today regarded as some "Disclosure worthy" conflicts – including Morgan's long-term relationships with Adlai Stevenson's presidential campaigns and the Democratic party, and especially including this fact: when Simulmatics was preparing its three major reports for the Kennedy campaign, the company's president, Ed Greenfield, arranged for Morgan to edit them. That's how he obtained and read them. Morgan of course may have foreseen that his article might be perceived as helpful by Greenfield and Simulmatics… this brings us to…

News-Flash… er… Cold-Water-in-the-face-Splash Two: Morgan's *Harper's* article did, in fact, fit beautifully into the Simulmatics business strategy. The company was happy to (if only by implication) take credit for electing Kennedy. Professor Lepore's just-excerpted section ends with this:

> "[Simulmatics president] Ed Greenfield didn't believe in bad publicity. This ruckus [Morgan's Harper's article and its aftermath] was just what he'd been hoping for. He [predictably?!] put Morgan on Simulmatics' payroll as its head of public relations. He intended to make an initial public offering of Simulmatics' stock."

Again – we need to ask – who is the puppet here? And is the puppet-master a person… or a robot?

News-Flash… er… Cold-Water-in-the-face-Splash Three: the Kennedy campaign… now the Kennedy Administration – was furious… and reacted… well… predictably -- their punch cards might have accurately described them as: "rich, ruthless, Eastern elitist, white male brass-knuckled politician." From Brass Checkers to Brass Knucklers -- they lied. The day the Morgan *Harper's* story hit the news-stands, Kennedy's Press Secretary Pierre Salinger put out a news release. Professor Lepore recounts (p 130):

"'An electronic brain designed to estimate voter reaction to campaign issues made strategy recommendations for Sen. Kennedy, it was reported Sunday,' according to the wire service story that ran the next day, December 19th. 'But the top Kennedy aides denied receiving or following the recommendations.' The piece quoted Salinger as saying (i.e., lying), 'We did not use the machine. Nor were the machine studies made for us.' This denial ran in papers all over the country…"

Having a continuing mainstream media discussion about the Simulmatics/Kennedy nexux could have been highly damaging to the incoming Administration. From the "extablishment" point of view, that simply couldn't be allowed – and it wasn't. The People Machine story faded as the mainstream media spotlight faded and turned to "newer news."

But it didn't disappear… not by a moon shot. To see this, let's start with a closer look at "The People Machine" – the January 1961 *Harper's* article by Morgan.

The article begins with a section in italic, introducing the "People Machine" idea. Here's an excerpt from that italic intro:

"Weather-machines" have been developed which react mathematically the way weather usually acts in reality. Vast quantities of carefully weighed past data – a model of the world's weather – are stored in the memory cells of a computer. When the current weather information is added, the weather-machine simulates future weather behavior and enables trained analysts to make long-range forecasts many times more reliable than older techniques of meteorology."

"Can something akin to these things be done where people are concerned? What if one could fuse the talents of the electronic computer – memory, speed, accuracy – to those aspects of human behavior revealed by public-opinion polling? What if one could devise a mathematical model of the American public and feed it into a

*computer? Wouldn't this be a 'people machine'
that could simulate future human behavior?"*

The Morgan *Harper's* article then proceeds into more
and very useful detail – here's another extended excerpt:

> "The model's basic premise was related to that
> of the science of public-opinion polling: People are
> predictable. Polling had reached a high level of
> accuracy in reporting the current distribution of
> opinion in the community. But Gallop and Roper
> had found individual behavior to be so sensitive
> that, as in the case of forecasting elections, polling
> had to be done as close to election day as possible.
> Therefore, polling was essentially static. Interviews
> could be punched on IBM cards, tabulated, and
> evaluated. Projections could be made with a small
> degree of error (e.g., the 1960 election projections).
> Yet polling could not get around the fact that each
> IBM card still represented an individual at a given
> moment in time. A poll could provide information
> on which a politician or a businessman could base a
> decision about the future, but nothing in a poll
> would project the change that might occur under
> new circumstances. What was needed was
> something that could simulate new circumstances
> and test the results of a decision before it occurred
> in real life.

"To break through the limits of polling, McPhee, Pool, and Abelson introduced the kind of speculations about human dynamics and change used by social scientists in their more creative and literary moments. [**Ed. Note**: in the next sentences "Middletown" refers to a series of sociological case studies based on research in an actual town – however the town's real name was replaced with "Middletown" which was to represent a kind of generic small city.] The Lynds, who wrote Middletown in 1929, in effect worked from a 'model' and used their own brains as computers. Their conclusions were far more than reports on the results of a survey. They tried to answer what if questions. They started with facts they had observed, organized, and tabulated, but then they attempted to 'compute' the nature of change. They made an effort to understand, given the facts, how people might behave in varying future situations.

"Now, using computer technology, the Simulmatics group was able to return, better equipped, to the dynamic method of the Lynds. They could lay out their own "Middletown" – a model of the electorate, the buying public, or the viewing audience – in the memory cells of a computer. They could use much of the data that had been so painstakingly collected by pollsters over so many years. With precision, speed, and efficiency, they could define groups in the population whose past behavior could be clearly identified and could permit the computer to play out alternative courses of events."

As noted, with a de facto order to from the Kennedy Administration to kill the story as mainstream hard news, the People Machine story quickly faded and flickered out.

But the underlying story – the reality -- didn't disappear – it just relocated to new venues. The Simulmatics corporation itself went bankrupt in August 1970. But the people who drove it during the 1960s had many incredible impacts. To start our brief review of those impacts, let's again roll out our highlighted Upton Sinclair quote: "**The social mind now has masters. Shrewd gentlemen sit in swivel chairs and consult with subordinates as to what tropisms they desire to have created; and either these tropisms are created, or the masterful gentlemen find more competent subordinates.**"

Simulmatics was in the business of providing "competent subordinates." But as Professor Lepore shows through her book, they had, at best, mixed success at this business. More specifically, the biggest opportunity – the one today's tech giants are all tapped in to today – was all kinds of commercial and mass consumer markets. Of course Simulmatics did try to serve commercial markets. But their primary competitors – giant advertising agencies – had vast data resources that Simulmatics lacked… and the ability to produce their own computerized means for implementing all kinds of automated applications of the "basic beans" Morgan had already spilled in his *Harper's* article. That article opened many doors for Simulmatics. But their lack of data combined with the inevitable mistakes people and organizations make in any new and exploding area of technology. As Simulmatics quickly lost the competitive advantage it started with the big ad agencies were ready to swoop and take over.

With the federal government contracts Simulmatics was better positioned. The government was itself the primary or exclusive supplier of data, the fact that Simulmatics had an up-and-running, well publicized computer model made them a top choice. And of course, we must consider the possibility that the Kennedy Administration "owed them." Unfortunately for Simulmatics, the inherent difficulty of doing anything so new was combined with almost-certainly unrealistic ideas about what could be accomplished. By and large, government agencies ended up being unhappy with their work. As to the unrealistic expectations – the Defense Department was hoping for a model that could predict when insurrections would happen around the world. Daniel Patrick Moynihan, later a prominent advisor to President Nixon and a Democratic Senator from New York, wanted a model that could predict when riots would occur. Failure and disappointment were probably inevitable.

Simulmatics was also involved in Vietnam, trying to process information about what was going on in hamlets, in an effort to "win hearts and minds"… another project probably doomed from the start.

I should briefly note here that various big ideas cooked up by the government from 1960 to 1970 and forward is being given limited attention here. This is really another major story line that should be developed – especially as it relates to potential U.S. and Western "interventions" throughout the former Soviet Union, and how such activity might be considered when viewing current events in Ukraine. More on this below.

One of the most important experts at Simulmatics, Ithiel de Sola Pool, the Political Science Department Chair at MIT, was heavily involved, along with others, in Defense Department work. As opposition grew to the war in Vietnam, he was accused of being a war criminal. MIT Linguistics Professor Noam Chomsky "led the charge" against Pool, who resigned under pressure as Department Chair – this was at a time when Professor Chomsky was rising to national prominence as an activist.

Looking at things now in the context of the Russian invasion of Ukraine, we need to take a broader look at an obvious, massive, and still-ongoing program by the U.S. to try to "interfere in everything big-time" all over the world

– using both Simulmatics (while it existed) and the mentality and approaches that derived from it. It seems more evident now that the entire Vietnam disaster can be traced directly to the kind of thinking that Simulmatics spawned. One question we should put on the front burner concerns the history of the collapse of the Soviet Union and its aftermath. Did we miss an historic opportunity to help Russia and the other former members of the Soviet Union to move in a far better direction than they ultimately went? Did the de facto policies of the West amount to simply a continuation of the kind of mentality of behavioral control and conditioning that ultimately led to the Vietnam disaster? We need to re-examine this entire history – going back to way before the original formation of the Soviet Union. And let's keep this in mind: one of the reasons the Soviet Union "dissolved" was established at the formation of the Soviet Union: a formal constitutional right of larger individual "Republics" – including Ukraine -- to leave. By contrast, the American Civil War established once and for all that individual states do *not* have a legal right to secede from the United States.

Amidst all of this, Simulmatics played a crucial role as both the originator of e-mail, and the internet itself, by way of their work at DARPA. They were also involved in something called the Cambridge Project, designed to plan the integration of government data resources at locations that, it was anticipated, the emerging internet would link into a single vast resource for all kinds of research and modeling.

In short, a lot of what we're concerned with today: especially big data and massive, controlling mega-corporations, was developing fast during the 1960s, and Simulmatics was right at the center of it all.

But beyond the insider business and political activity, the Simulmatics storyline also continued to be visible to the "public mind" – and in a typically American way – as fiction. A continuing but fiction-based narrative of American history is a long-standing tradition. Upton Sinclair's <u>The Jungle</u> was not news reporting – it was a novel. America's discussion of all kinds of challenging topics, including of our Civil War and Slavery, has always been carried on as much in fictional venues as in "hard news" and "hard history" – <u>Uncle Tom's Cabin</u> and <u>Gone with the Wind</u> are two of the most famous examples. Children's books should also be considered in this category. Because they were often read aloud by parents to their children, they can be seen as having content at two levels – and as a way for writers to spread political ideas outside of the venues of newspapers and magazines. <u>The Wizard of Oz</u> is a perfect example of this. The "adult" content woven into it was centered on the controversy between a Gold-only standard and a Silver standard – in the title, Oz actually is the abbreviation for ounce – the unit of measure for precious metals. American political discourse has long been sublimated (and suppressed?) in this way.

The Simulmatics story went forward in the same way. The original Morgan *Harper's* article was by a well known popular "free-lance" journalist – the quotes are needed because of his undisclosed conflicts. But another major participant in the real Simulmatics corporation was Eugene Burdick, a fascinating character in his own right, and a Simulmatics insider (but not a stockholder) whose involvement Professor Lepore carefully sleuths out. Burdick was a Rhodes Scholar, a Berkley political science professor, a famous author, and "the Ale man" – a celebrity featured in ads fo Ballantine Ale. His books included <u>The Ugly American</u> and <u>Fail Safe</u> before he rolled out <u>The 480</u>, (1964) -- his fictionalized hybrid story about Simulmatics. The book project started out in 1963, tangled up with what was to be a made-for-TV movie called The Candidate – a film with that name was released in 1972 starring Robert Redford. Because Berkley had sold the movie rights, and was appalled by how his script was re-written, when <u>The 480</u> was published there was no chance of making it into a movie. As Professor Lepour recounts, although the book itself is fictionalized, it draws heavily on what Simulmatics really did in 1960 – the book even includes an appendix listing the 480 voter types Simulmatics identified, and as for the text, Profess Lepore reports: "Burdick lifted whole passages straight out of Simulmatics reports and memos." (p 185.) But of course, in the wake of the Kennedy Assassination, and with no movie version, the impact of Burdick's novel on the "popular mind" was limited.

To conclude the "book review" aspect of this topic, Professor Lapore's book is a valuable and fascinating account of a company that history had "lost sight of," although its activity was central to the events of a crucial time period in the development of technology. Her book is also reminiscent of Upton Sinclair's writing, the "dead hand" books in particular, in its thorough interweaving of background on the personal lives, marriages, families, social networks and "fictionalized parallel universes" of the principal people involved. Many sociological and cultural insights are offered up, as important elements in a tapestry of lives and events that are often slighted or neglected in earlier historical accounts – which have of course typically been written by men.

However, by way of criticism, the treatment of Republicans generally, and Richard Nixon in particular, strikes me as marginal, harsh, and as having none of the depth of knowledge and nuanced understanding Professor Lepore so obviously has regarding people that frankly seem more representative of the social and academic world she lives in. Of course the relatively brief consideration of Republicans generally can be accounted for by the fact that the Democratic Party, and Democratic candidates, had both taken the lead on the attempt to build a People Machine, and were in control of the Executive branch of the Federal Government throughout the brief operational life of Simulmatics.

We should note one final point: At the beginning of the Kennedy Administration the Morgan People Machine article in *Harper's* was potentially the beginning of a Watergate-sized scandal – if the whole "Corpica Establishment" had wanted it to grow into one. But… they didn't. Theodore H. White's groundbreaking <u>The Making of the President 1960</u> doesn't mention it. Many eyes were on the prize: there was a whole "New Frontier" to open up… with lots of opportunities for the whole Eastern elite "family" – and all kinds of agendas, from political, to business to personal – to "entertainment."

As we proceed things will get *more* unscientific… not less. Here are three "behavioral science" issues that we must try to think through as best we can.

Issue One - the possibly-to-apparently successful attempt of the 1960 Kennedy campaign to control aggregate political behavior by means of Simulmatics – the "People Machine." When we look back now on B.F. Skinner, and how critics engaged with his activity, one aspect that I find central is a kind of failure to engage directly with what Professor Skinner seems to have been up to in this sense: His critics concentrated on the idea of something approaching a total ability to control human behavior – to the point where a person literally has no "free choice" in anything – everything can be both predicted and determined. Of course, it's easy to refute this, simply by providing the example that a person can formulate and articulate two possible choices in many given situations, and can then consciously choose one over the other by a exercise of a "free will" that is difficult to impossible to disprove.

But as we've seen with the Simulmatics example, there is another way of thinking of a "behavioral science" approach to controlling human behavior – in the aggregate. The strategies formulated in actual Simulmatics reports to the Kennedy campaign are really nothing less than case study examples of how behavioral science *was* used to attempt to control the aggregate behavior of an entire country. After all, the premise of the whole Simulmatics operation was that, in effect, hypothetical "public opinion polls" could be conducted regarding future circumstances that were within the power of the Kennedy campaign to shape. From the campaign's point of view, the desired behavior was of course the behavior of the electorate in "choosing" Kennedy. But… so goes the logic… this "choice" could possibly be, and possibly was, controlled by how the Kennedy campaign approached two crucial political issues: the race issue and the religious issue.

Looked at this way, in the aggregate rather than on a person-by-person basis, the idea that human behavior cannot be controlled looks a lot weaker. Could the idea of controlling individual, personal behavior have been a kind of "straw man" argument that was deliberately put up by the "behavior controllers" to distract from their real objective – developing a technology and a practice of controlling not individual personal behavior, but aggregate political behavior?

Issue Two -- specific but vast. As we've see, Simulmatic did try to get into the business of using "behavioral science" to "control" consumer behavior. They were thwarted by their competitive disadvantage regarding access to data – the big ad agencies had it and they didn't. In terms of the sheer size of the market this was orders of magnitude more vast than the political and electoral domain they started in. The big ad agencies quickly developed software that could compete with Simulmatics.

The real question here is trying to understand what we might think of as a "Corpica controlled environment" – one in which the combination of behavioral science techniques developed by the Skinner cohort and the modeling and predictive techniques pioneered by the Simulmatics cohort, have been systematically combined over decades. Big Data is the operative buzz word today – representing the potential of giant corporations to more and more relentlessly control what "consumer choices" are offered. The **DO** part of my **DO GET USE** approach is my best effort to try to address this challenge.

Issue Three -- there has been a steady increase in the power and technique of a bi-partisan establishment of Corpica control of "America" -- which (sadly) it now seems appropriate to put in quotes. Corpica, in turn, is composed almost entirely of college graduates, with a high concentration of graduates of elite colleges, who are "products" of a culture of behavioral conditioning. They've been molded and stuffed with Skinnerian ideas. If a person is going to survive within this culture they must internalize a world view. "Political correctness" only begins to describe it. And here's where we come full circle with Upton Sinclair. The behavioral culture of his adult life up to his run for Governor was in his view dominated by large business organizations with a determination to install a culture of consumerism and conventional "what's good for business is good for America" thinking. But in the intervening period I think the dominant ideology of the Corpica culture has shifted to something much more in alignment with Professor Skinner's thinking – and "Simulmatics thinking." I conclude from this that the whole analysis of the process of controlling a culture that Upton Sinclair documented at length is still valid – but the "values" – "beliefs" – whoever or whatever is "pushing the buttons" of all the behavioral technicians working with that culture -- has changed. The result that I see is a dominant Progressive Institutional Authoritarianism that simply and effectively "cancels" anyone who tries to work within it but does not behave according to its "values" – "beliefs"… whatever.

Then… along comes Trump… claiming "I alone can fix this." And here's the thing: it's easy enough to conclude that he's *right* to have said that he was the only person who *could* and *would* take on this army of elite Corpica behavioral engineers. He established a reputation… well… an image… of a successful businessman who could and did thrive in a Darwinian world. He had enough money (who knows how much) to enter into the political system in 2016. And he was uniquely able to, in effect, co-opt the mainstream media environment by giving it the one thing it craves – eyeballs.

There's a concept in politics called "earned media." This is a dollar valuation of what someone would pay to obtain the same exposure of people to their ideas – more to the point the *image* they're *selling* – that media provides in the form of "news coverage." I've seen reports that in the 2016 campaign the economic value of Trump's "earned media" was about $6 billion. That's more than both President Obama and Governor (now Senator) Mitt Romney spent together in their 2012 campaign.

But Trump has gone further. He has organized – and for practical purposes enculturated -- a critical mass of the electorate in such a way that it can no longer effectively be reached by the pre-Trump "media establishment." This "Trump counter-culture" simply repels and rejects a worldview, or a "mainstream culture," that, from my point of view, the currently dominant Progressive Institutional Authoritarian culture of America is insisting we all must accept. We now have what amounts to a bi-polar media environment.

This is what I perceive as our current political and cultural environment, and what I'm seeking to change with my campaign. In the simplest terms: I reject the attempts at enculturation of *both* Progressive Institutional Authoritarian America *and* of former President Trump and his followers.

It's time to end this chapter (!) – by summing up my view of all this and what I propose should be done about it – again with a series of bullet points and subpoints:

- Explain and advocate for **DO GET USE** – of course this has already been presented in detail in chapters 3 through 6. Just three sub-points should be highlighted here.

  - **First**, I have deliberately designed **DO GET USE** to be appealing to Republicans and Trump supporters. If you're going to try to convince people to change their beliefs, you must offer something that is better. I'm trying to do this.

  - **Second**, more specifically, I believe the **DO** part – **Demand Organizing** – is a practical way of bringing about major changes in our society with only a permissive role for government – action (and spending!) are to be avoided unless there is a broad based consensus for it. All we ask is that at a minimum government get out of our way. As noted earlier, in cases where there is a consensus for a more positive and active role for government, I'm not opposed in principle for working along those lines, and this includes potential government-organized capital at the state level. However, any use of government money must be in the context of a plan for paying back the government in full over some period of time. The government must have a senior security interest in all the equity and assets of any Public Benefit corporation that is being advanced capital. In other words, I don't think we should ever plan on having government assume a continuing and/or open-ended role in financing anything in the **DO GET USE** framework.

- **Third**, I have also deliberately designed **DO GET USE** to be broadly appealing to people of different political and ideological beliefs – including Democrats, the "woke Left" and Socialists. I don't see any reasons why in principle people with diverse political views and values can't work together on many projects in the **DO GET USE** framework.

- Raise awareness of how everyone is being behaviorally conditioned and controlled – Of course this whole chapter has been considering that ad nauseum. But I believe this needs to be an "up front" constant theme in all political discourse. Our cultural environment has become so poisoned that we must be constantly appealing to everyone to consider what "brand of messaging" they are being subjected to – and to consider that *all* purveyors of political messaging -- sometimes AKA "news and information" -- may be presenting things in an incomplete and/or distorted way. Isn't it better to try to listen to a range of different points of view, and to then try to find value and common ground in those different points of view? We must be especially aware of how utterly dependent all "mainstream media" is on "capturing eyeballs" for revenue and profit. **Note:** So-called "non-profit" media is just as much a part of Corpica as for-profit media. And by the way, all media now appears increasingly to be seeking direct sources of government funding – this is part of new spending being proposed by the Biden Administration.

- There may be an opportunity for a Liberal-Conservative alliance… a "resistance" against *both* Corpica and Progressive Institutional

Authoritarianism. Once, decades ago… there was such a thing as a "Liberal Republican" (I may be the last one left.) Let's think for a moment of a Western movie set and a metaphorical – m e t a p h o r i c a l -- "high noon" three way Liberal/Conservative/Progressive shootout. Our default scenario – the one that I see Corpica as promoting – is that Progressives can just fold their arms, smile, and wait for the Liberals and the Conservatives to finish each other off. But there is an alternative to consider. One of the core ideas of traditional liberalism tends towards libertarianism. In terms of the explicitly liberal <u>A Theory of Justice</u>, a foundational exposition written by Harvard Professor John Rawls, we are asked to think of "Justice as Fairness" as having two ordered principles. First: everyone should have the greatest liberty consistent with an equal liberty for everyone else. Second: inequality in the distribution of basic goods to different representative groups of people is just if the people in the "worst off group" are better off than they would have been in a society ordered according to different principles. In other words, envy, or having less, is not a good reason for saying that a society is unjust. Let's leave aside for a moment possible critiques of this theory, and focus on the point that "equal liberty" as a priority value has traditionally been viewed as a *liberal* principle. By contrast, let's consider what today is characterized as a "cancel culture" – in which the whole idea of diversity of viewpoints is being challenged. Both Progressive Institutional Authoritarians and Corpica can be seen as allies in a program of suppressing all but a set of viewpoints they deem to be acceptable. If we view things this way, there may be an opportunity for both traditional liberals and today's conservatives to unite within the Republican party under a common banner of challenging the cancel culture mindset of both Progressive Institutional Authoritarianism and Corpica. Of course there is room in this big tent for libertarians. The point is that we need a common acceptance that there is a diversity of ways of looking at the world -- and that our first challenge is to ensure that there is liberty in discussing our differences openly, without trying to suppress anyone's participation in our economic life, or our politics and culture, based on what they believe. This is conditioned only on a commitment not to advocate or accept violence. Let's leave it here for this long-winded bullet point.

America needs a "media truce" – "Turn Off, Tune Out, Drop In"

This phrase is the "theme slogan" of my campaign – to be featured on buttons and bumper stickers. The three two-word phrases are each the exact opposite of a "theme slogan" advocated for by Harvard Psychology Professor and psychedelic drug guru Dr. Timothy Leary: "Turn On, Tune In, Drop Out."

Both Professor Skinner and Professor Leary were psychologists, and both were on William F. Buckley's Firing Line, (enter "Buckley Leary Firing Line" in the youtube.com search box.) But they were more or less polar opposites in the field of psychology. Rather than concentrating on behavior and ignoring any notions about Freedom, Dignity and subjective ideas about human consciousness and experience, Dr. Leary wallowed in ideas about subjective experience. He was a de facto advocate for the use of drugs like LSD, and did not dispute Mr. Buckley's introduction of him in a 1967 edition of Firing Line: "Dr. Timothy Leary is the Pope of what he chooses to call a new religion, which is based on the consumption of drugs, particularly, at the moment, LSD, whose attractions are said to be sweeping the campuses and after whose initials Dr. Leary has named this new religion the League for Spiritual Discovery."

Responding to Mr. Buckley's question: "Why is it that the common impression is that poorly adjusted people tend in greater numbers to the world of LSD than normally adjusted people?" Dr. Leary said: "the people who are using marijuana today tend to be the highly educated. They come from our so called best colleges {cross-talk} there's no LSD or marijuana problem down in Podunk Junior College in Arkansas, it's at Harvard, Princeton and Yale that 50% to 70% of undergraduates are seriously experimenting with the most important thing that can be experimented with: their own consciousness."

Professor Leary made a distinction between what he thought of as "consciousness-raising" psychedelic drugs like LSD, and alcohol. Briefly falling silent at one point after a question involving Podunk University, he told Mr. Buckley: "No, I'm trying to see what your problem is and I think I've diagnosed it." [Buckley: "Go ahead doc"… laughter] "Your approach to the word 'drug' I think is that of many Americans, particularly over the age of 50, who when the word 'drug' is mentioned think of some opiate… something that is an escape, something that takes you away from reality, something that you take if you're a failure. All of the statistics that I've seen indicate that the people who use psychedelic drugs are people who are pretty well adjusted by any standard of criteria you want to name: income, education, creativity, productivity, and they want more. Because what psychedelic drugs produce is not the dull, glazed, three-martini haze. Psychedelic drugs intensify consciousness, they're microscopic in their effect, and they're used by people who are looking for more."

Dr. Leary goes on to suggest: "You can actually live, you can make love, you can enjoy food, you can raise children, without being a computerized, medicated American." Professor Leary also said -- possibly for legal "plausible deniability" -- that he did not advocate using drugs. But his whole presentation was more or less a litany for why people might want to practice his new religion.

Professor Leary also characterizes himself as "more conservative" than Mr. Buckley, talked about "media guru" Marshall McLuhan, and foresaw an emerging electronic and media age. As a personal response to all of this, I remember thinking in Washington D.C. in 1973, where I was working as an intern in Republican Congressman Bill Frenzel's office, that America seemed to be heading for an age of "conservative hedonism." Disclosure: at age 19 I had no problem obtaining a supply of marijuana in Washington D.C. at that time. With a one day exception I haven't used any drugs other than alcohol and coffee since my mid-twenties – I almost never have more than two drinks, maybe once or twice a year, and don't drink at all most days. Drinking is not a consciousness-raising or religious experience for me… I just like the buzz.

Thinking of "drugs" generally as "consciousness-raising" or "consciousness-affecting" experiences, it's difficult to not think of all of our gadgets as some kind of "drug-equivalents." Professor Leary seems to have been thinking along this line.

In today's COVID world of distance-everything, media saturation, and personal isolation, today's most physically dangerous drugs are opioids, including the synthetic fentanyl. Opioids caused over 75,000 of the over 100,000 drug deaths in the one year ending April of 2021. But our gadgets, and our media, while less fatal, seem to really be America's primary "drug of choice" today. And our incredible national division is one major side effect of this national addiction.

This is why the "theme slogan" of my campaign is the flipped-over version of Timothy Leary's. I'm saying we should all:

- **"Turn Off"** your devices -- They are drugs. Media is a drug. Money is a drug. Read a book. Listen to music (I make music an exception to the general "no devices" rule.) Go for a walk, or take other exercise. Do all the things we can do *without* our devices.

- **"Tune Out"** – Don't watch or listen to programming that makes money by dividing us.

- **"Drop In"** – Go visit someone.

It's that simple. We can literally turn off and tune out America's incipient Civil War 3. This is my suggestion.

12 – OUR "MINNESOTA NICE" POLITICAL TRADITION – HUBERT HUMPHREY AND AL QUIE

One of Minnesota's historical political advantages is the fact that over the decades our politics has often (not always) been relatively free of personal rancor. Our last Gubernatorial campaign was in 2018 – one of the bitterest national elections in recent memory. But in Minnesota our two major party candidates continued our historical tradition – they got along well personally, although clashing more pointed late in the campaign. When conceding defeat on election night, Republican Jeff Johnson wished Governor-elect Tim Walz success, and he meant it.

Vice-President Hubert Humphry is another great example of how politics can avoid becoming personal – and also of what widespread public support a person can win in a partisan election. After losing the Presidency in 1968 to Richard Nixon, Hubert Humphry was returned to the U.S. Senate. Chuck Slocum, in his 20s when elected to chair the Minnesota Independent Republican party (renamed after Watergate) remembers "76 in 76." That was both the year Hubert Humphrey was re-elected to his second post-Vice-Presidential Senate term, and the vote percentage he won. A big part of Vice-President Humphrey's success is that he was a "people person." He loved people, he really connected with people, and he had an incredible memory of all the people he met.

A few weeks before he died of cancer in early 1978 Vice-President Humphrey called former President Richard Nixon, and invited Nixon to his funeral. Nixon, who had defeated Humphrey in 1968 and had resigned in 1974 due to Watergate, accepted. Humphrey's funeral marked the beginning of Nixon's re-emergence into public life.

Of course history and politics did not stop. Due to Humphrey's death, both U.S. Senate seats and the Governorship were on the ballot in 1978. Nationally, 1978 was the last election in 44 years when a President whose party controlled both houses of Congress held on to both houses. That's certainly a cautionary fact for Democrats in 2022. In 1978 Republicans gained six Governorships, three Senate seats, and fifteen House seats. In Minnesota, Republicans won both U.S. Senate seats and the Governorship.

Al Quie, a Congressman since 1958, was elected Governor. He is a deeply religious man, and continued the

Minnesota tradition of keeping political and partisan disagreements from becoming personal. His biography, <u>Riding into the Sunrise: Al Quie: A Life of Faith, Service & Civility,</u> by Mitchell Pearlstein, recounts one meeting that Gov. Quie attended in Northern Minnesota with the State Senate Democratic (DFL) leader – who Quie invited to come see him in his office when they were back in our Saint Paul capital. When he dropped in, Gov. Quie said he just wanted to tell him "I love you." When then-Congressman Quie was asked by Charles Colson to ask President Ford to pardon Colson, he declined – reasoning that another Watergate pardon would lead to Ford's defeat. But later, Quie called Colson's lawyer and offered to personally serve the rest of Colson's prison sentence – something that legally can be done. Colson declined.

This is how Minnesota politics has worked for many years. It's a tradition that Minnesota politicians know about. It's badly frayed recently, but it's still here.

13 – I WILL WORK TO KEEP TRUMP OFF ANY FUTURE FEDERAL BALLOT

This is like "who will bell the cat?" Some poor mouse has got to step up and do it. I'm volunteering.

It's important to be realistic. Right now Donald Trump is still *the* dominant force in the Republican party – as harmful as this may be. But he suffers from something that catches up eventually with everyone who doesn't die young: Age.

On Inauguration Day 2017, Donald Trump was seventy years old – the oldest person ever to be sworn in as President.   On January 20th 2020 President Biden broke that record by a country mile – he was 78 years old. If either President Biden or former President Trump is sworn in on January 20, 2025 they will break that record again – Biden by exactly four years, Trump by only about half a year. If Secretary Clinton were to run again and win, she would be 77 when sworn in; at sixteen months younger than Trump she would not break the record currently held by Biden.

Here's the reality that we can easily miss from these comparisons: *all* of these people are *way* too old to be President. Not a little bit too old – *way* too old.

But this presents us with an opportunity – something I'm advancing as "The Compromise of 2023" – a Constitutional "band-aid" that could in a relatively benign way stop the world's oldest Constitutional Republic from being run – or doddered over -- by the world's oldest governing cohort. Below is my plan, rendered in newspaper commentary format… I'm going to keep promoting this opportunity. The title refers to the "Compromise of 1850," which for all its flaws did *delay* America's Civil War – what I call "Civil War 2" -- for a decade. Here's the plan:

The Compromise of 2023

by: Bob "Again" Carney Jr.

In the wake of the first anniversary of January 6, 2021 battle lines for the 2024 election are already becoming more and more fortified. Democrats are accusing Republicans of putting our elections and institutions under siege. The Biden Administration and Democrats are being accused by Republicans of hyping January 6th because "It's all they've got" – followed by a litany of alleged "Biden disasters." Discussion is out in the open now about Hillary Clinton's possible candidacy. Talk of an American Civil War is in the air.

Trump v Clinton 2024 would be the first "Presidential Grudge Match" in our history to drag us back not one but two election cycles.

Fortunately, we can both head off such a dangerous rematch and fix what is ever more apparent as a glaring Constitutional flaw. Let's amend our Constitution to establish a maximum age limit for our President.

To start this process, let me suggest a short, simple amendment text – designed to be broadly acceptable and fully adequate. Alternative texts can emerge… but let's give top priority to understanding the compelling need to start a discussion. Presenting "The Compromise of 2023" -- Amendment XXVIII:

A person becomes permanently unable to exercise the powers and duties of the office of President on their 75th birthday. A President-elect 75 years or older on inauguration day shall permanently fail to qualify as President.

That's it… short and sweet (a line saying Congress can enact enabling legislation could be added.) This could be Constitutional law before the 2024 primary process has chosen any national delegates for either party.

There is a precedent for fixing a "Constitutional bug" before the next election. The original Constitution gave each Elector two undifferentiated votes. In 1800 everyone "knew" that Thomas Jefferson was "supposed to be" the Presidential candidate on his ticket. But when he and his running mate Aaron Burr tied in the Electoral College our Constitutional machine kicked in – a tie vote automatically threw the election to the House. The Twelfth Amendment established separate Presidential and Vice-Presidential Electoral ballots in time for the 1804 election.

Amendment XXVIII could head off a *Trump v Clinton* "grudge match" in 2024.

More generally, this amendment would force our political process to refocus on candidates who have the (relative) youth and energy to serve two full terms as President.

Obviously, there are all kinds of ways of improving on this text (it's phrased based on some existing but non-intuitive Constitutional language.) But right now – today -- we can't ignore a serious, already-bleeding and fast-worsening wound to our "body politic." Granted, the proposed Amendment XXVIII text amounts to a kind of "Constitutional band-aid." But we should view the "band-aid" character of the text as a feature, not a bug. We can best head off disaster if we don't try to get too fancy or accomplish too much.

If a national XXVIII debate proceeds, more comprehensive and more thorough Amendments will be proposed. Great! We should seek out more and better ideas. But we must not let the perfect be the enemy of something that is both good and needed.

To be blunt: we must head off the possibility of electing Trump as President in 2024. Beyond the proposed Amendment XXVIII other ideas and approaches are possible. However, because the brief and mechanical Amendment XXVIII avoids naming anyone, it is our most benign option.

We should be open about the fact that Amendment XXVIII is intended to be a compromise. Let's be clear about the fact that it would Constitutionally cancel a "2024 worst case scenario" for both many Democrats and many Republicans.

I'm calling on all office holders and candidates to either explicitly endorse the proposed Amendment XXVIII text, or to offer a comparable alternative. Let's begin an urgently needed discussion on this.

As noted this plan is benign in the sense that it doesn't actually name anyone – but the people it would be most likely to affect are of course obvious. The great advantage is that it does begin to address, however imperfectly, a problem that has become obvious, and needs to be addressed. There is an opportunity after the 2022 election for both parties to unite behind this – partly for the practical reason of heading off a "Grudge Match" –

but also to send a clear signal that it's time for a new generation of American leadership. I'm hopeful and optimistic that this idea might gain enough support to happen.

But returning to my stated objective – I believe it is essential to America's well-being that former President Trump *must not* appear on an election ballot again. There is a real possibility that more than one alternative Republican candidates will emerge by 2023, each with prospects of successfully campaigning for the nomination. In the still-likely event there are Republican majorities in one or both houses of Congress, I think that this could actually help that effort a lot. A new policy agenda could begin to advance in Congress – looking for a President who would sign into law what is being proposed.

Still… I'm not convinced GOP leadership will be enough to ensure that someone else can win the 2024 Republican Presidential nomination. However, if President Trump is convicted in a Judicial trial on one or more charges related to what I believe was an insurrection on January 6th, 2021, that could disqualify him -- both legally as a practical political reality.

The most likely violation that would disqualify former President Trump seems to be 18 U.S. Code § 2383 - Rebellion or insurrection. Here's the text (emphasis added):

> Whoever <u>incites, sets on foot, assists, or engages in any</u> rebellion or <u>insurrection against the authority of the United States or the laws thereof, or gives aid or comfort thereto</u>, shall be fined under this title or imprisoned not more than ten years, or both; and <u>shall be incapable of holding any office under the United States</u>.

The claim is that while President, Trump incited the violent occupation of the U.S. Capitol on January 6th.

There is one area where I believe I can make a contribution to this debate. In the next couple of months I'll be publishing a book presenting a Constitutional theory I've been working on since 2000. The main application of this theory to our current situation is that I think I can show that if the House has impeached someone, *Congress* can present the case *directly* to the Supreme Court, mandating an original jurisdiction criminal trial. This is a relatively new wrinkle on an overall theory I've been advancing for over 20 years. Following are two almost-never-considered passages from Article III of our original Constitution. Here's the first:

> *The Trial of all Crimes, except in Cases of Impeachment; shall be by Jury;…*

Two points are especially important. **First** (and now obviously, since you just read it) *"Cases of Impeachment"* is an explicit Constitutional phrase. And of course, what else could a criminal *Case of Impeachment* be but a case involving a person who had been impeached? **Second**, an impeached person loses their right to a jury trial according to this provision. It could be argued that the Sixth Amendment re-introduces this right for an impeached person – but I personally find the argument showing that it does not to be both complicated and persuasive. But for now please simply consider this: doesn't the idea of a single Judge, with no jury, deciding on a case involving someone who was important enough to be impeached seems strange? Yes... it does. That's why this first provision leads us to consider a second, immediately preceding passage regarding jurisdiction with one phrase underlined for emphasis:

> *In all Cases affecting Ambassadors, other public Ministers and Consuls, and those in which a State shall be Party, the supreme Court shall have original Jurisdiction. In all the other Cases before mentioned, the supreme Court shall have appellate Jurisdiction, both as to Law and Fact, <u>with such Exceptions, and under such Regulations as the Congress shall make</u>.*

This was a big issue in the most famous and decisive case in Supreme Court history: *Marbury v. Madison* (1803.) In that case Chief Justice John Marshall's opinion concluded the Supreme Court could not issue something called a writ of mandamus ordering then-Secretary of State James Madison to deliver a judicial commission, because in his view the Supreme Court only had appellate jurisdiction over the case, but the underlying law provided for issuing the writ in a Supreme Court original jurisdiction action.

Here's a key point: in his opinion, Marshall ignored the underlined passage, which in my view, based on the text we just looked at, specifically empowers Congress to make *exceptions* to the general division between original and appellate jurisdiction. Notice also that according to my theory Congress can make exceptions on a case-by-case basis, and specifically with reference to *"Cases of impeachment."* In *Marbury v Madison* Congress had made an exception to the original division of jurisdiction not with a reference to a specific case, but by a law of general application. I think these are arguably two distinctly different circumstances.

Here's more of my argument: The most obvious need for such an exception regarding jurisdiction would be the criminal trial of a *Case of Impeachment.* This is why I believe Congress, by a joint resolution – notice that no *law* is required because obviously an impeached President probably wouldn't *sign* it! – can *mandate* that the Supreme Court, acting as an original jurisdiction trial case, must try a current or former President who had been impeached for an alleged violation of criminal law. The alleged criminal law in question would of course be the one cited above -- 18 U.S. Code § 2383 - Rebellion or insurrection.

Continuing further with my argument, I believe that if the House of Representatives' Select Committee investigating the events of January 6th 2021 determines there is probable cause to try former President Trump under 18 U.S. Code § 2383, then Congress may, by joint resolution, cite the House's Article of Impeachment as a Presentment to the Supreme Court for an original jurisdiction criminal trial. In that joint resolution, Congress could provide explicit and specific regulations for how that one specific trial was to be conducted. The regulations could specify time limitations for the length of the trial; who would prosecute it (possibly the Attorney General personally); that a majority vote of the Court would be sufficient for conviction; and that there will be no jury. Finally, the regulations could provide for the option of a postponement of the judgment phase of the trial. This is a separate phase of a trial that occurs after conviction. Here's the key point: while the judgment phase can be postponed regarding the length of a sentence and a fine, the restriction preventing former President Trump from holding future office would be effective as an immediate consequence of conviction.

This approach offers four great advantages. **First,** having the Supreme Court hold the trial recognizes how important the question is. **Second,** because there is no appeal, we won't have to wait for months or years, i.e. until after the 2024 election, to know for sure whether or not former President Trump is disqualified from holding office. **Third,** this is the best option we have for resolving the legal issues concerning former President Trump and January 6th 2021, including the months leading up to it — in a *non-political forum.* **Fourth,** this would force us to fundamentally rethink the question of whether a President is above the law – and how a President can and properly should be held accountable to obeying the law.

By the way, as to the Supreme Court's postponement of judgment, I don't see any reason why judgment can't be postponed until *after* the 2024 election. A fine is required, but I wouldn't see probation as necessarily an inappropriate sentence. Let's listen to the better angles of our nature.

As for *Marbury v Madison*, for now let's just keep in mind that for whatever reason the underlined Constitutional passage regarding "such exceptions" was ignored in Chief Justice Marshall's opinion. I don't know of any Supreme Court precedent for a case that turns on that passage. Let me be clear that there are problems here – this will require more study and analysis. But the bare fact that the passage *wasn't* any part of the *Marbury v Madison* opinion is very important – as is the fact that no writ of mandamus is involved in the situation we're now considering. In short, it seems reasonable to argue that *Marbury v Madison* is *not* a point-on legally controlling precedent for the issues being raised here.

A third and related possibility has been raised – former President Trump could be disqualified from holding federal office, including the Presidency, based on a provision of the 14th Amendment: no one can "hold any office, civil or military, under the United States," who "shall have engaged in insurrection or rebellion against the same, or given aid or comfort to the enemies thereof." Congress can remove this disability by a two-thirds vote. There is an on-going debate over whether or not this Amendment provision is self-executing, and if it is not what is needed for it to apply to any particular person.

I list this third possibility because it is so obviously related to the previous scenario – the original jurisdiction Supreme Court trial. It seems possible if not evident that the Statute cited: 18 U.S. Code § 2383 - Rebellion or insurrection, was drafted with the 14th Amendment in mind. More to the point, that statute makes disqualification to hold Federal office automatic on conviction – so there is no question of how the 14th Amendment's disqualification provision would be carried into effect.

This third approach can also be acted on by State Legislatures, who, per the Constitution, have authority to determine the "manner" in which Electors are chosen, from Article II, Sec. 1:

> *"Each State shall appoint, in such Manner as the Legislature thereof may direct, a Number of Electors, equal to the whole Number of Senators and Representatives to which the State may be entitled in the Congress: but no Senator or Representative, or Person holding an Office of Trust or Profit under the United States, shall be appointed an Elector."*

Notice the phrase "may direct." Of course you could argue that the Legislature may direct this process by passing a law. But as with the question of appellate vs original Supreme Court jurisdiction, no reference is made to law. From this I conclude that Governors need not be involved in this Constitutional process – a State Legislature does not have to pass a law regarding the selection of Electors. Instead, I argue that similar to my proposed approach for an original jurisdiction Supreme Court trial, both houses of a State Legislature can simply pass, by a majority vote in each chamber, a joint resolution prohibiting the selection of Electors supporting Donald Trump, based on the premise that because he has "engaged" in insurrection the 14th Amendment disqualifies him from being the President. Simple as that. I'll be proposing this at the Minnesota State Legislature this session.

As noted, sometime in the next few months I'll be publishing a book that presents a comprehensive and new (in the sense that it is almost unknown today, but not new in the sense I've been working on it for over twenty years) – specifically in the context of the insurrection of January 6th, 2021, and specifically addressing the how, why and consequences of a Supreme Court original jurisdiction criminal Trial of former President Trump. In the meantime, my book <u>Break Glass Impeach Trump</u>, published in 2017, is available on Amazon, and will shortly be a regular free download from my website.

Some concluding "Trump Phenomena" bullet-points

- With the recent Russian invasion of Ukraine we have now see clearly how the danger that Vladimir Putin personally represents has come full circle. But we need to revisit the question of interference in the 2016 U.S. Presidential election by Russia and Putin beyond and outside of the question of "collusion" or conspiracy involving the Trump campaign. The bare fact of Russia's interference has long been well known – this was in fact the topic of the first of the two major parts of Special Counsel Robert Mueller's 2019 report. While Mueller cleared the Trump campaign of legal issues related to collusion or conspiracy, he emphatically demonstrated that massive Russian interference did occur – with the specific intent of electing Trump. Looking back we now see how similar this undertaking was to the participation of the Simulmatics Corporation in the 1960 U.S. Presidential election. In both cases I believe a strong argument can be made that the"but for" test can be met: "But for [Simulmatics project / Russian interference] President [Kennedy / Trump] would not have been elected." However let me also suggest this: of these two cases, the case showing successful Russian/Putin interference in 2016 is probably stronger than the 1960 case of Simulmatics and Kennedy. We can and must now raise the issue of whether the 2016 U.S. Presidential election was on a de facto basis "stolen" by Russia and Putin.

- Going forward we must also focus more directly on what has long struck me as a disturbing pattern: *both* in his gambling casino activity and in his selling of condos – Trump's basic business model seems to be clearly predicated on providing what amounts to providing "money laundering as a service." A casino operation offers people the opportunity to buy chips for cash, and then cash them in for a check, which can of course be deposited in a U.S. bank. What happens in between – whether the chips are gambled or not – is irrelevant. The point is that rather than depositing cash in a bank, a person or a business is now depositing a check. Similarly with the business of selling condos – it has been reported that the Trump Organization has sold many condos to various murky purchasing entities, which could enable the use of funds obtained in corrupt ways by all kinds of Russian and other oligarchs. Once a condo is owned, its title can be transferred in various ways. When the same condo is eventually sold, payment has typically been made by check – the result is a "clean" financial transaction at the tail end of a series of earlier transactions that can be impossible to audit. In short, the whole business of transacting condos can be seen as largely or almost entirely a giant money laundering scheme. It's been well documented that Trump's businesses have relied heavily on financing outside the convention financial system relied on by most businesses. As we go forward, and the Trump Organization faces a growing threat of being unable to obtain the professional services of lawyers and accountants, he may become increasingly dependent both for financing and professional services on what may be emerging as an entire financial and legal system that is de facto separate from the current international system – and that may be controlled by Russia, China, and other authoritarian states. All of this cries out for more investigation and reporting.

- As noted, Trump is still very powerfully in control of the Republican Party – but he appears to be flying "under the radar" in this sense – he's cut off from Twitter, and the mainstream media doesn't report very much on his activity. However, a de facto alternative media has emerged – and he has attracted large crowds at two recent January rallies, one in Arizona and the other in Texas. The upshot of this is that he is almost certainly energizing the Republican base, without attracting much notice or attention – so most people aren't aware of his ongoing impact.

- Few people understand the crucial importance of the Trump organizations' dominance of both state Republican parties, and the infrastructure of professional Republican political operatives. As a practical matter this means no GOP office holder can really stand up to Trump. At best, by occasionally muttering something about "inappropriate"… by remaining mostly silent… and by occasionally declining to restrict their future options, they can suggest Trump may face competition if he runs for the nomination in 2024.

- Trump's issues agenda is both in tune with the GOP base, and is also frankly something I am personally sympathetic with in many ways. However… as a separate question I'm personally not sure whether Trump himself actually believes anything. He certainly has an instinct for "what sells." My issue with Trump are not primarily about specific policies – rather my focus is centered on how obviously divisive, dishonest and corrupt he is, and with either his lack of understanding or his fundamental refusal to accept, basic ideas about the limited powers of a President, and how the institutions of a "small r" republican form of government is intended to function. It would be dangerous for him to again be able to "exercise the powers and duties" of the office of President. His dishonesty and corruption may have made the Republican party irredeemable –

as part of my consideration of that possibility I recently read <u>It was all a Lie</u> by Stuart Stevens, who presents a powerful indictment of the modern Republican party. But we are on the horns of a dilemma – there are also huge issues and problems with the Democrats.

- With some specific exceptions I have until the invasion of Ukraine still been generally in favor of the Republicans winning both houses of Congress in 2022. There needs to be a check on the Biden Administration. In 2018 I support voting for Democrats for Congress across the board for the same reason. Beyond that, I think having the ability to take policy initiatives would pave the way for other GOP candidates for President to emerge. But beyond this, I think it could result in a whole series of needed Congressional investigations about issues that in my view are being suppressed and downplayed by both the Democrats and what I see as the "Corpica-media establishment." These can be and should be undertaken on a bi-partisan basis. However, given the Ukraine situation my general inclination favoring the election of Republicans to Congress this fall is subject to change.

- Minnesota's Mike Lindell – the "MyPillow guy" – has emerged as a major force in Trumpworld. He played a prominent role in both of Trump's January rallies. He appears to have turned MyPillow into a

business directed squarely at the Trump base –
selling directly to them and heavily advertising on
Fox and other increasingly-politically-aligned outlets.
It's simply impossible to know at this point what
future national political role he might play.
However, in Minnesota Lindell is clearly positioned
to be a "Trump Enforcer" if he chooses to do that.
I don't think there's any question he has both the
constituency and the financial resources to enter the
Minnesota GOP primary for Governor as the
leading candidate – regardless of what the State
Convention might do. Consider that in 2018 Bob
Anderson – a kind of "Trump stand-in" – won
about 36% of the vote for the U.S. Senate seat held
by Tina Smith… with a low-budget campaign
against Convention-endorsed State Senator Karin
Housley. Trump voters that Anderson inspired to
vote in the primary may have provided Convention-
endorsed Jeff Johnson with his margin of victory
over former Gov. Tim Pawlenty. If any
"establishment" GOP candidate for Governor
moves their big toe away from Trump's party line,
Mike Lindell could probably demolish them in a
primary. **Note**: the Russian invasion of Ukraine
could have an impact on what is presented in this
bullet point – it's too soon to tell about that.

- As suggested in the second bullet point, recently (as
  of mid-February 2022) Trump is facing what

appears to be mounting danger on legal fronts –
greatly increased by a letter from Mazars, the Trump
Organization's accounting firm, saying the Trump
financial statements for the last ten years "should no
longer be relied on." Mazars has terminated its
relationship with Trump and the Trump
Organization. Trump has also been ordered by a
New York Judge to testify within three weeks in a
civil deposition regarding the New York Attorney
General's fraud investigation of the Trump
Organization. Both his son Eric and the Trump
Organization's accountant, Allen Weisselberg,
reportedly took the Fifth Amendment over 500
times during depositions in 2020. Here's the key
point: any organization of the size and complexity of
the Trump Organization simply cannot function
without the services of lawyers and accountants. We
may be reaching the point where, *as a profession*,
lawyers and accountants will no longer work for the
Trump Organization. As a matter of practical
business considerations this may be a de facto death
sentence. Alternatively, we might see some entirely
new financial and legal system emerging from
Russia, China and the Middle East. Note: as with so
many things now developments in Ukraine are an
unknown factor here. But we should not discount
possible financial and even professional resources
that may be available to Trump from an entire
corrupt network of Russian and other authoritarian

regimes. We must consider the possibility that the Trump Organization may be restructured in ways that move major management and accounting activity of its business offshore. The global business environment is obviously changing rapidly and unpredictably.

- Regarding the dominance of state parties by the Trump organization and political operatives, it's important to identify a second Minnesota-specific aspect to this. Currently a major GOP operative, Tony Lazzaro, is in jail awaiting trial on sex traffic charges involving minors. His arrest directly resulted in the resignation and replacement of GOP State Chair Jennifer Carnahan – who had been associated with him. One aspect of this situation merits specific consideration; it's been reported that when his home was raided, almost a million dollars of gold bullion was seized, along with a lot of silver bullion. While there is no conclusive evidence that I know of at this time, this suggests to me that he may have been involved in the production and sale of Trump Gold Coins. This brings us to the next bullet point.

- One of the unusual aspects of the Trump post-Presidency is the emergence of a commercial market for all kinds of Trump-branded gold and silver coins. I think this needs to be studied and investigated – however, I'm not certain what information about the production and distribution of these products may be available. **Important Note:** a recent *NY Times* article reports this is generally in the hoax category, so this bullet point and the general danger of Trump-branded precious metal "private label" physical currency might be a false alarm – however the NY Times article did not mention the Disme company – which had been prominently featured for the Trump rally in Arizona. Beyond the simple need for an investigation, I think we must also consider that Trump-branded gold and silver coins might emerge

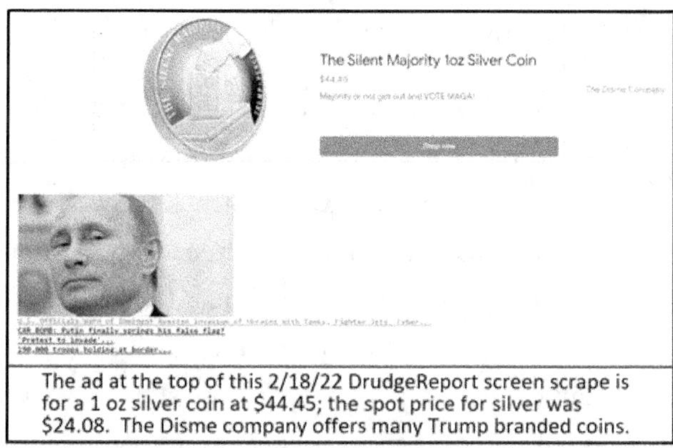

The ad at the top of this 2/18/22 DrudgeReport screen scrape is for a 1 oz silver coin at $44.45; the spot price for silver was $24.08. The Disme company offers many Trump branded coins.

as a kind of "private label" currency. It seems possible that retailers might start to accept these coins as payment for merchandise and services. Of course we've also seen this emerge with crypto-currency. In short, from the point of view of "hard metal advocates" – is there a need for the Government to "go back to the gold standard" if gold and silver coins can be produced and used privately? At this point I just want to identify this as something that could become an issue going forward. Above is an example of an advertisement that appeared on DrudgeReport.com on Friday, February 19th, 2022. We should note that while counterfeiting U.S. currency is a crime – producing "fake" versions of what we could call "private label" precious metal coins isn't in the same legal category – it would almost certainly be some kind of fraud – but it wouldn't be counterfeiting per se. At any rate – this whole "potential racket" could be so problematic that it's possible Trump was at one point involved, but is no longer involved.

- One final bullet point on the Ukraine situation. Russia currently exports about seven or eight billion barrels of oil daily. China is Russia's biggest customer. However, recently China has been importing a total of about 10 billion barrels of oil a day. Here's the point: it's possible that world import-export patterns could be shifted in a way such that countries moving to cut off Russian oil imports would simply be re-directing more of Russia's production to China. In short – if Russia and China really do have a solid alliance, then Russia could sustain its current export market, and more generally could sustain its economy by maintaining its overall level of export of all fossil fuels, regardless of what the West does. Just another piece of the puzzle to consider.

To sum up: my priority is to ensure that Donald Trump *never appears* on a Federal election ballot again. As Winston Churchill once said: "I don't care *how* you do it… you must sink the Bismarck." Of course… we're not talking here about "sinking Trump." I personally don't have any objection to ultimately letting him live out his days playing golf at Mar-a-Lago. My concern is that he *must never be President again.* If we can ensure that, over time his political career might come to be seen as one that included both many significant positive contributions – but was fatally poisoned by his dishonesty, corruption, and authoritarian alliances -- and demonstrated the danger of misunderstanding the power and purpose of the office of President as badly as he and others did… and still do.

14 – "BE PREPARED" – RICHARD PAINTER AND AN EMERGENCY GOVERNOR'S RANKED CHOICE BALLOT

University of Minnesota Law Professor Richard Painter is emerging as a prospective piece in the 2022 Minnesota Gubernatorial puzzle. He is a former ethics lawyer in the Bush Administration, who has emerged as a strong critic of President Trump and his legal and ethical challenges. Most recently he has filed for the Democratic primary for the Minnesota First Congressional District special election – as noted I have filed for the Republican primary in that election.

We should also note that another person – former TV and Radio personality Cory Hepola, has announced he is running for Governor under the Forward Party banner – that party was founded by Andrew Yang, who was a Democratic candidate for President in 2020. For the rest of this chapter, Hepola's emerging candidacy should also be considered when we're examining the possible impact of Professor Painter's candidacy for Governor.

In 2018 Professor Painter ran in the Democratic primary opposing Sen. Tina Smith, who was running in a special election for the last two years of former Sen. Al Franken's term – Franken had resigned after being accused of groping women. There never seemed to be any real prospect that Painter would win – but as an anti-Trump former Republican the 78,000 votes he received probably included a significant number of voters who would otherwise have voted in the Republican primary. Those votes would likely have gone to former Republican Gov. Tim Pawlenty, who had been critical of Trump, rather than to the Republican Convention-endorsed Jeff Johnson, who was firmly allied with Trump. Many were surprised when Johnson defeated Pawlenty by about by about 28,000 votes. Late in the 2016 campaign, after the "Access Hollywood" tape emerged and briefly appeared likely to force Trump to be replaced as a candidate, Pawlenty had called Trump "unhinged, unqualified and unfit." Pawlenty was widely thought to be potentially a stronger general election candidate than Johnson.

Beyond possibly impacting the GOP primary for Governor, if almost all of Painter's votes had also gone to Gov. Walz -- the most conservative of the three major DFL candidates in the primary – that might have also have put Gov. Walz over the top. In short, there is reason to think Professor Painter might have been running in the DFL Senate primary at least in part for tactical political considerations – to encourage a shift of moderate Republicans towards the Democrats.

However, this is speculation. Sen. Tina Smith was Gov. Dayton's Lt. Gov. for two years. She was not well known. Professor Painter had a strong resume and significant policy differences with the incumbent – both were valid reasons for thinking he could raise a significant war chest and mount a successful challenge.

But this year he's talking of running for Governor without major party support as a candidate on the general election ballot. Gov. Ventura only barely made it in a three-way race, under unusual circumstances. Given our current system of voting it's almost impossible to see how Professor Painter could anticipate mounting a serious challenge, especially with an incumbent Democratic Governor in the mix. We can speculate as to how his candidacy could affect a three way race, but let's not attempt this.

Instead, if Professor Painter does go ahead, we should consider how voters – that's us – could take the initiative and demand some form of Ranked Choice Voting – including by a deliberate planned campaign to mark the existing ballot to show their choices, and then demanding that the intent their ballot clearly represents be fully recognized and counted – which could only happen if ballots were effectively counted as Ranked Choice Ballots.

Assuming Professor Painter does go ahead with a campaign for Governor — and this is not yet certain — I plan to raise the issue of how we can accommodate to a three-way or four-way race for Governor in the General Election. I think we must reject the idea that Government has any right founded in principle to, in effect, censor *our* free speech — and voting is our ultimate exercise of our Constitutional right to free speech .

I won't elaborate further on what prospects there may be here. I only seek to raise this as a prospective issue in this year's election.

AFTERWARDS – FROM DISUNBRATIONISM TO TRUMP… TO HUNTER BIDEN… TO THIS BOOK'S PROSPECTIVE REVISED COVER… AND BEYOND?

The current book cover may be a temporary one – the explanation of that is below. Briefly, there are seven images on the cover. The first is a reproduction of Upton Sinclair's post-election book about his 1934 campaign for Governor of California. The second is a cover image of a pamphlet from the 1960 Kennedy campaign – even way back then they were publicly on to the perceived threat computers represented: taking people's jobs. Of course as Chapter 11 recounts in detail the Kennedy Administration went quickly into cover-up mode regarding allegations that they used computer simulation technology to win the election. The third image is of something positioned as a kind of educational robot – as you can see, it's about the physical size of a kindergarten student. This product is from www.eduporium.com – it's currently being sold for

$12,990. Robots are now mainstreaming everywhere, including in education. The fourth image is an Electoral College map of the 2016 Presidential election – highlighting three states (WI, MI and PA) that Trump won by less than 1%, and a fourth (FL) that he won by 1.2% The fifth image is the cover of the Mueller Report, released in 2019 and documenting extensive interference by Russia and Putin in the 2016 U.S. Presidential election. It's overwhelmingly clear that the Russians had a clear preference for electing Trump. It seems highly likely that but for the Russian interference Trump would not have won. The sixth image is of people climbing up the U.S. Capitol building on January 6th, 2021. The seventh image is a map showing the state of Russia's invasion of Ukraine as of about March 10th.

Things are frankly long past the point where we need to soberly consider whether the current division and turmoil in America politics is, in fact, an intended result of actions of both Russia and China – actions that appear to have continued into the Biden Administration… possibly premised on an ongoing preference both of those nations have for the "brand" of authoritarianism Trump continues to represent and advocate for.

Why the cover might be temporary: Towards the end of <u>Money Writes</u> Upton Sinclair recounts what appeared to start out as a kind of "practical joke" of one his friends, but then morphed into a kind of case study of how arbitrary "schools of modern art" can be. The wife of his friend, Paul Jordan, was a realistic painter who wasn't getting much recognition from critics of the time. Mr. Jordan decided to "take up brushes" against this holier-than-thou papal-smearing see of critics – although he had never painted before, he rounded up some oil paint, and painted up… something-or-other… then naming it "Aspiration." He hung it up in his house, and said nothing.

Let's tune in now to Sinclair's own account of this (p 191):

> "…presently his friends began to stare and ask questions. Paul Jordan, in his spirit of waggery, began to take it seriously; he evolved his 'spiel' about the 'cosmic rooster' and the 'law of dynamic symmetry,' and he found that, in the parlance of the advertising experts, it 'went over.'
>
> So then he decided to become an international figure, and invented the romantic 'Pavel Jerdanovitch," with the Russian birth and the life among the cannibals. He had photographs of himself taken, dark and ferocious of aspect, and wild of eye. He painted three additional horrors – one called 'Exaltation, portraying the exctasies of a native damsel who summons up the courage to defy the tribal taboo and eat the sacred banana; another called 'Adoration,' portraying a savage worshiping a piebald boa-constrictor in Alaska, and a third called 'Illumination,' because it is

made up almost entirely of eyes. 'Exaltation' was crated and shipped to New York, where it was shown at the Independent Exhibits, in the Waldorf-Astoria Hotel, March, 1925, and solemnly discussed by the critics, and made the subject of an elaborate article in a Paris art journal, 'Revue du Vrai et du Beau,' September 10, 1925, page 18. The picture of the washerwoman and the cosmic rooster was shown at the 'No-Jury Exhibit,' at Marshall Field's, in Chicago, January-February, 1926; and in the 'Art World' of Tuesday, January 26, you will find a feature article, proclaiming this as the most brilliant exhibit of many moons."

And so on. You get the picture.

Not only does history sometimes repeat itself… it looks like History may be getting into the business of numbered limited editions

The mainstream media has recently informed us that President Biden's son Hunter has taken up art. He is now reported to be selling his art – something that's perfectly legal – many artists have long been known to do this.

Type "Hunter Biden Artist" in Google search box and you may be brought to something from https://news.artnet.com/art-world/hunter-biden-gallery-show-1979790 with this 300 words of excerpted content (The Google search title is "We Spoke to Hunter Biden About His New Life as a Full-Time …"):

… The topic of our interview has nothing—and yet everything—to do with Biden's well-documented struggle with addiction, his new memoir, his famous dad, his made-for-the-tabloids romantic life, or his ties to President Trump's impeachment and to Ukraine.

… While he has no formal training, Biden has been making art since he was a child. In recent years, the practice has taken on a more formal, serious turn and he now works as an artist full-time. He has a dealer, Georges Bergès; a studio; and a collector base. A solo show is on the horizon. Bergès plans to host a private viewing for Biden in Los Angeles this fall, followed by an exhibition in New York. Prices range from $75,000 for works on paper to $500,000 for large-scale paintings, Bergès said.

…Working on canvas, metal, and Japanese Yupo paper, Biden's artworks are often layered, with elements of photography, painting, collage, and poetry. Some are geometric abstractions, filled with patterns and somewhat hallucinogenic. Others depict trees, leaves, and body parts like outstretched arms.

'I don't paint from emotion or feeling, which I think are both very ephemeral,' Biden said. 'For me, painting is much more about kind of trying to bring forth what is, I think, the universal truth.'

It's tempting to brush off a statement like this as a bunch of malarkey. But for Biden—a controversial figure who has been vilified by the right and uncomfortably ignored by the left—what is that universal truth, exactly?

'The universal truth is that everything is connected and that there's something that goes far beyond what is our five senses and that connects us all,' he said. 'The thing that really fascinates me is the connection between the macro and the micro, and how these patterns repeat themselves over and over.'

According to TheHill.com, "Hunter Biden's controversial art gallery show draws fierce critics," Nov. 11, 2021, Shirin Ali:

The *New York Post* weighed in on Biden's New York exhibit:

"The *New York Times* recently reviewed Biden's debut solo exhibition, titled "the Journey Home," which consisted of two dozen paintings. Biden described his artwork as, 'literally keeping me sane,' as he struggled with various alcohol and drug addictions."

Ethics concerns arose over the summer about Biden's artwork and the White House created an agreement with Bergès to keep purchases confidential, according to the Washington Post. The agreement allows Bergès to set prices for the art and withhold all records, including potential bidders and final buyers.

Bergès also agreed to reject any offer that he sensed to be suspicious or that was above asking price.

But some have been critical of the whole agreement, with Richard Painter, chief ethics lawyer to president George W. Bush, telling the Post that, 'the whole thing is a really bad idea. The initial reaction a lot of people are going to have is that he's capitalizing on being the son of a president and wants people to give him a lot of money. I mean, those are awfully high prices."

University of Minnesota Law Professor Richard Painter figured prominently in Chapter 14 – this whole ball of wax might become an issue in the 2022 Minnesota Governor's race.

Of course it's hard not to wonder about how all this may tie in with the new "LSD religion" Professor Timothy Leary was promoting – as we considered in Chapter 11. Hunter Biden's statement that his artwork was 'literally keeping me sane' sounds believable to me on its face.

I visited the Bergès website and had a look at some images of paintings. Given our review of the review by "experts" of the artwork of Upton Sinclair's friend Paul Jordan, I'll pass on the opportunity to offer any critique of it. I don't have any reason to deny the possibility that there is some sort of a spiritual dimension involved in this example of what Upton Sinclair would almost certainly call "MammonArt." But that doesn't mean he is spiritually in a good place. The nexus of politics… corporate cash… international relations… creativity… "experiments with consciousness"… an insular, elitist, privileged "higher" educational environment… this sentence could go on and on! Here's my own frank and "low expectation" conclusion: It's obvious to me that Hunter Biden is a troubled person. Maybe Timothy Leary warned him but he just didn't listen. If his art career… or "art career"… with or without quotes… brings him some money, has a therapeutic benefit in the sense of helping him to "not lose his mind," and at least kinda-sorta detaches him from real, genuine, dangerous disasters like his involvement with Ukraine and Burisma… something that also cries out for more investigating… maybe that's the best we can hope for. This cries out for more investigating.

All of this reinforces my own conclusion that Joe Biden should *not* be the President and the Democrats should *not* be running things. I voted for Biden in 2020, and advertised this plan in a bunch of small Star Tribune Sunday ads that ran statewide before the GOP U.S. Senate primary. It was the only way to ensure Trump would not be the President. OK… mission accomplished. But there have been side effects. Now… one of my priorities is to ensure *Biden* will *not* be re-elected. I've got a long list of priorities!

A brief mention should be made of "Painter of Light" Thomas Kincaid. He was a commercially successful artist, but also the driving force between a kind of "art-as-a-business" model. Rather than go into any detail now – let's just note that going forward both Kincaid's work as an artist and his ways of commercializing his art – including the employment of assistant artists, may become topical. Kincaid was apparently an alcoholic; he died at age 52, in 2012 after drinking and consuming valium.

Meanwhile, opportunity seems to be knocking here.

That's why this book cover might be replaced – with anonymous artwork signed: "Jerdanovitch-Bidenski" (the full name is P. H. Jerdanovitch-Bidenski; bio to follow.)

You might even be able to get a numbered limited edition print. And of course… since Jerdanovitch-Bidenski is anonymous… there's always the subcontracting option. Stay tuned!

www.ingramcontent.com/pod-product-compliance
Lightning Source LLC
Chambersburg PA
CBHW061628250726

48659CB00004B/1130